AF488042

HUMANITY'S EVOLUTION OF INNER STRUGGLE

THE SAPIEN PARADOX

SHIBAM

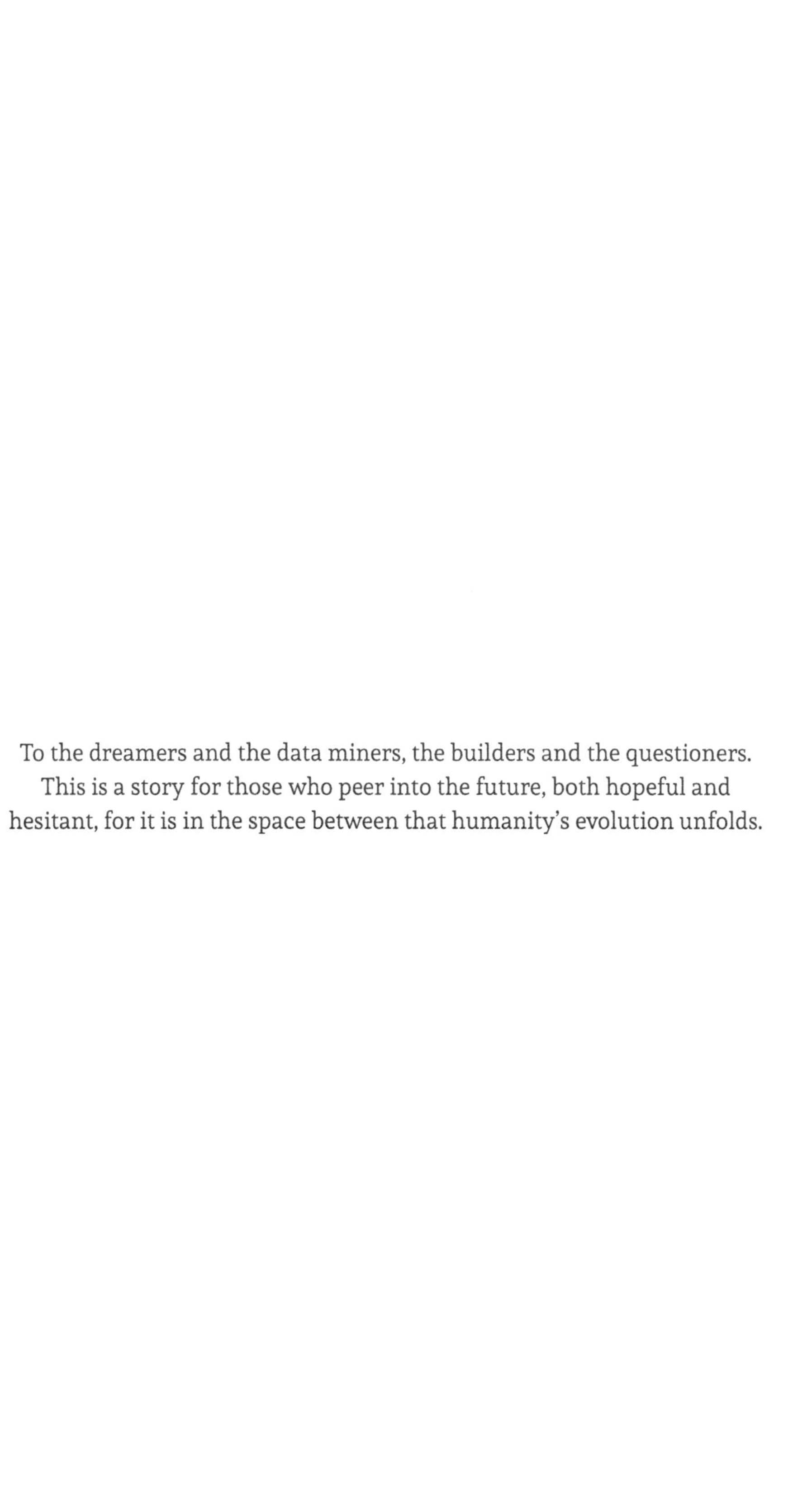

To the dreamers and the data miners, the builders and the questioners. This is a story for those who peer into the future, both hopeful and hesitant, for it is in the space between that humanity's evolution unfolds.

Contents

Contents

PREFACE

From the moment we first cracked open a coconut with a rock, humanity has been locked in a continuous struggle. Ever wonder why we humans seem wired to worry? Our greatest wars are often fought within ourselves. It's almost as if the more we explore the potential of artificial intelligence, the more we grapple with our own internal complexities.

Are we even making our own choices anymore? Maybe AI is secretly pulling the strings behind the scenes, nudging us in certain directions without us even realizing it. Traffic jams will be a thing of the past, because super-smart AI will control the flow of cars. Shopping will get easier because AI algorithms will predict what you'll want to buy before you even know it yourself.

Data, for all its precision, is ultimately an imperfect mirror reflecting a messy reality. In this meticulously ordered existence, anomalies and paradoxes exist, and they appear like a flawless facade.

Black holes exist and not even light can escape through it. Similarly anomalies exist within rigid logic of the data sets, based on which random deviations will occur in the Artificial Consciousness of future systems.

Acknowledgements

This journey into the "_Humanity's Evolution of Inner Struggle_" has been a collaborative effort, and I owe a debt of gratitude to many who helped bring this story to life.

First and foremost, thank you to my readers, the dreamers and the skeptics alike. Your curiosity fuels my passion for exploring the complexities of our world.

I am also grateful to my family and friends for their patience and understanding during the long hours spent wrestling with this story. Your unwavering support provided the foundation upon which this book could be built.

Prologue

There was a time when I believed books changed the world.

Perhaps they do.

But years later, I have come to suspect that books change their authors first.

Every book begins as a question.

A small discomfort in the mind.

A loose thread that refuses to stay tied.

Most people learn to live with such questions. They raise families, build careers, fall in love, grow old, and allow the mystery to remain.

A few choose differently.

They follow the thread.

What begins as curiosity slowly becomes obsession. Years disappear into notebooks, conversations, journeys, failures, relationships, philosophies, religions, sciences, and dreams. Entire seasons of life are traded for the possibility of understanding something that may never be fully understood.

This book was born from one such question.

Not why civilizations rise and fall.

Not why technologies evolve.

Not why nations compete.

But why the greatest battles in human history have always mirrored battles taking place within the human mind.

Humanity crossed oceans because of curiosity.

Built empires because of ambition.

Created gods because of meaning.

Waged wars because of fear.

Loved because of belonging.

Dreamed of immortality because it knew death awaited.

Every age appears different on the surface.

Yet beneath every revolution, every religion, every ideology, every technological breakthrough, and every personal decision lies the same invisible landscape.

The inner world.

This is the story of its evolution.

Not the evolution of our bodies.

Not the evolution of our machines.

But the evolution of our struggles.

For years, I believed this book would provide answers.

Now I think questions matter more.

The pages that follow are not conclusions. They are observations gathered while wandering through the oldest frontier humanity has ever known.

The mind.

Because despite everything we have built, conquered, discovered, and imagined, our greatest mystery remains unchanged.

The endless evolution of the human inner world.

The end of one story.

The beginning of humanity's next question.

Part I – The Primal Divide

I

Whispers In The Dark

The laboratory should not have existed.

Yet there it stood beneath the outskirts of Lisbon, hidden behind abandoned warehouses and sealed railway tunnels long forgotten by official maps.

The investigators entered cautiously. The facility looked less like a research center and more like the remains of a battlefield.

Server racks had been dismantled.

Hard drives had been melted from the inside.

Storage units had been physically crushed.

Whoever had come here last had not been interested in theft.

Inspector Rafael Mendes had spent twenty years investigating organized crime, political corruption, and cyber-terrorism. Nothing about the scene felt familiar.

The tactical team entered first, weapons raised. The facility stretched farther than he expected. Glass-walled offices overlooked central workspaces large enough to house hundreds of researchers. Notebooks lay open where their owners had left them. A jacket still hung from the back of a chair in one corner.

The deeper the team moved into the facility, the stranger it became. According to municipal records, the underground structure did not exist.

According to satellite surveys, the land above had remained abandoned for nearly a decade.

According to government databases, no institution had ever been licensed to operate beneath the site.

A technician approached Rafael carrying a tablet.

"We found something."

"What survived?"

"One file."

Rafael frowned.

"One file?"

The technician nodded.

"Everything else is gone."

The file originated from a system labeled only:

MNEMOSYNE

No further explanation accompanied it.

No institutional logos.

No project references.

No ownership records.

Only a timestamp.

Sixteen minutes before the disappearance of Dr. Shivam Sen.

Rafael stared at the timestamp.

The name meant little to him, but he recognized the world that had produced it.

The old order had begun changing long before anyone noticed. The COVID-19 pandemic had exposed how fragile global systems could be. The rise of large language models after the public release of ChatGPT in 2022 had triggered an international race for artificial intelligence. The war tensions between the United States and China increasingly revolved around semiconductors, computing power, and control of data.

By the late 2020s, intelligence agencies, universities, and technology firms were all asking variations of the same question:

How much of human behavior could be predicted?

The world's most valuable companies were no longer competing only for markets. They were competing for attention, data, and models of human decision-making. Every click, purchase, message, and search became part of a growing map of human cognition.

Some journalists compared it to the nuclear race of the twentieth century.

Others called it the cognitive race.

The recovered archive contained thousands of documents, but one folder appeared again and again throughout the records.

Subject: Dr. Shivam Sen.

The name surfaced everywhere.

Research papers.

Internal audits.

Behavioral reports.

And a book.

The *Sapien Paradox.*

At first Rafael assumed it was another behavioral study. Then he began reading.

The facility had been investigating a controversial idea: that human decisions could be predicted long before people became aware of making them. Every movement, purchase, conversation, and hesitation left behind patterns. With enough data, the researchers believed those patterns could be used to forecast future choices with unsettling accuracy.

Most subjects fit the models.

Shivam did not.

His file was filled with annotations, revisions, and contradictory predictions. The system repeatedly failed to anticipate his decisions. What should have been routine became one of the laboratory's longest-running investigations.

The anomaly had begun years earlier.

Most of the supporting files had been erased, but The *Sapien Paradox* phrase appeared repeatedly throughout the surviving reports.

No definition accompanied it.

Only references.

Cross-references.

Warnings.

And thousands of pages that no longer existed.

Rafael added the title to his notes and continued reading.

Most of the surviving records converged on a single period in Shivam's life.

Not the publication of the book.

Not his recruitment into Mnemosyne.

Thailand.

The final entry concerned a cycling expedition along the coast of Thailand.

Researchers had given him a customized smartwatch connected to the Mnemosyne network. Officially it tracked performance metrics. In reality, it continuously streamed biometric and behavioral data back to the facility.

The route was simple: one thousand kilometers from Bangkok to Phuket.

For weeks, the system followed his progress.

Heart rate.

Sleep cycles.

Route choices.

Moments of hesitation.

The model was attempting to understand not where he would go, but how he thought.

According to the records, Shivam reached 963 kilometers.

Then the data became strange.

His pace slowed.

The watch recorded prolonged periods of inactivity.

Several voice notes were attached to the final transmission.

The transcripts showed increasing confusion.

Shivam repeatedly questioned the maps he was carrying. He claimed the coastline no longer matched satellite imagery. Villages appeared where none should have existed. Roads ended without explanation.

Then came the final entry.

"There should be land ahead."

A pause followed.

"There isn't."

The transmission ended there.

Sixteen minutes later, every record connected to the experiment stopped simultaneously.

And sixteen minutes after that, according to the timestamp on the recovered archive, Dr. Shivam Sen disappeared.

At the Promthep Cape in Phuket

II

Loops That Read You Back

The problem with anomalies is that they rarely stay isolated.

Inspector Rafael Mendes spent the next three days reading.

The archive was fragmented, corrupted in places, and written by dozens of researchers who seemed incapable of agreeing with one another. Yet certain details surfaced repeatedly.

Not equations.

Not predictions.

Stories.

Researchers documented recurring patterns in human lives that appeared across cultures, generations, and continents.

A woman who spent twenty years searching for her biological father only to discover he had lived three streets away for most of her childhood.

A soldier who survived a war because he missed a train after stopping to buy cigarettes.

A scientist whose career began after taking the wrong bus during a rainstorm.

The incidents themselves were ordinary.

Their frequency was not.

Mnemosyne referred to them as return loops.

Paths that seemed random while they unfolded but appeared inevitable when viewed in retrospect.

The concept sounded philosophical until Rafael reached the statistical appendices.

Millions of lives had been analyzed.

Relationships.

Careers.

Travel histories.

Medical records.

The researchers believed human beings moved through reality much like rivers moved through landscapes. Individuals experienced choice. The system observed currents.

People drifted away from certain places for years only to return to them.

Ms. Gupta? This is Dr. Kail from the Institute. You signed up for the cognitive augmentation study last month?"

The recording lasted barely three minutes.

Rafael almost skipped it.

Among thousands of interviews and participant logs, someone had flagged this call for preservation.

"Yes, I remember," a woman replied.

"Before we begin," said Dr. Kail, "have you experienced any recurring events recently? Places, conversations, people you keep encountering unexpectedly?"

"You mean coincidences?"

"No," she said. "Loops."

A pause.

"There is one thing. I keep meeting the same man."

"Where?"

"The first time was at an airport in Delhi. A year later, a bookstore in Singapore. Then a train station in Prague. Then a hospital waiting room in Mumbai."

"Did you know him?"

"No."

"Did he recognize you?"

"I don't think so."

"Then why did you remember him?"

Another pause.

"Because every time I saw him, he was reading the same book."

The transcript ended soon after.

Attached to it was a note:

Subject identified the individual four years later at her wedding. The man was the groom's cousin.

Probability estimate before encounter: 0.000004%.

Loop classification: Confirmed.

Rafael opened the video archive.

The recording was dated eight years before the facility's disappearance.

What Rafael discovered next explained why half the archive had been erased.

Shivam's anomaly was not the only reason Mnemosyne tracked him.

Years after joining the project, he published a book.

Within months, internal analysts began treating it as a security concern.

Behind a thick glass partition, researchers huddled around a projection. It displayed Shivam's original manuscript—banned in five countries after it was discovered to induce dissociative states in susceptible readers. Not with hypnosis. Not with images. Just with language.

"Page 88," one of them said.

The projection froze.

"That's where it starts."

"Starts what?"

Nobody answered immediately.

Finally, a researcher spoke.

"The readers stop knowing which thoughts belong to them."

Nobody in the room seemed surprised.

That was what caught Rafael's attention.

As the meeting continued, one name appeared again and again in the discussion.

Dr. Aditi Banerjee.

Rafael opened her notes.

Most were routine observations.

Dates.

Interviews.

Statistical anomalies.

Then the tone changed.

The entries became personal.

At first, Aditi assumed she was seeing patterns where none existed. The irony wasn't lost on her. She worked at Mnemosyne, where finding patterns was the job.

The first incident involved a pen.

A colleague, Mariam, often joked that Aditi borrowed pens and never returned them. One evening, Aditi found a pen with Mariam's name in her drawer. The problem was that she clearly remembered returning it.

Weeks later, similar incidents followed. Conversations felt familiar. Articles seemed pre-read. Faces lingered in memory without explanation.

Individually, they meant nothing.

Together, they resembled something Mnemosyne had spent years studying.

Loops.

Not in the world.

In perception itself.

Her insomnia began soon afterward. She woke with phrases repeating in her head, thoughts that felt borrowed rather than her own.

Around the same time, she began reviewing reports on The *Sapien Paradox.*

Seventeen countries had banned the manuscript.

Aditi skimmed the internal assessments and dismissed most of them as bureaucratic paranoia.

Books did not alter belief systems.

People did.

She closed the file and returned to work.

A week later, she began dreaming in voices she didn't recognize.

The symptoms appeared gradually. At first, Aditi blamed exhaustion. The investigation had consumed months of her life, and sleep had become increasingly difficult. But the headaches persisted. She woke at odd hours with fragments of conversations lingering in her mind, as though someone had been speaking just beyond the edge of memory.

Around the same time, she developed a strange habit. Every night, she found herself returning to a Turkish audiobook version of The *Sapien Paradox.* She did not speak Turkish. She understood almost none of the words. Yet she kept listening.

The waveform appeared normal.

Then Aditi overlaid the Turkish, Bengali, and Japanese versions.

She expected three unrelated patterns.

Instead, the major pauses appeared in nearly identical positions.

Not identical.

Close enough to bother her.

Her stomach tightened.

That shouldn't have been possible.

Something in the cadence disturbed her. The pauses felt deliberate. The rhythm seemed designed rather than spoken. Worse, listener surveys repeatedly described the narrators as unusually trustworthy, even when participants could not explain why.

She checked another file.

Then another.

The Turkish narration emphasized pauses.

The Bengali version amplified rainfall and street noise.

The Japanese recording carried faint echoes resembling temple acoustics.

Within eight months, the Turkish edition outsold state-funded curriculum titles. The Bengali audiobook reached 2.3 million plays. In Japan, rumors spread that a monk had taken a vow of silence after listening.

But no one saw the strings.

That night, she opened a Hindi paragraph from Volume III: The Mirror Mind. It read like poetic philosophy on first glance. But on re-reading, she noticed rhythmic refrains, like sonic tripwires:

"Tum the, tum ho, tum rahoge... par kya tum jaante ho kaun ho tum?"

She recorded the line and compared it against speech-pattern datasets used in Mnemosyne's cognitive studies. The rhythmic structure repeatedly clustered around intervals associated with meditative and highly attentive states.

Not enough to demonstrate intent.

Too much to dismiss as coincidence.

Next, she opened the French edition.

In a chapter titled "Ce que vous appelez réel", Shivam had constructed entire dialogues using embedded negatives:

"Il n'est pas faux que ce n'était pas un rêve."

("It's not untrue that it wasn't a dream.")

The layered denials weren't just linguistic games—they created cognitive load, forcing the brain to resolve impossible truths. Readers would feel clarity while absorbing contradiction. Confusion disguised as enlightenment.

Then English. So subtle it was nearly invisible.

He used abstraction as a weapon. Sentences like:

"Reality occurs where attention converges."

or

"You are the equation pretending to solve itself."

Vague. Profound-sounding. But neurologically, they mimicked what Aditi now called "semantic mirroring." The brain, desperate for coherence, would insert its own context, projecting meaning—and reinforcing it as belief.

But Bengali?

That one hurt.

Aditi thought she knew their texture. Their cultural weight. But Shivam had sliced through them with surgical precision.

He'd taken lullabies. Rain metaphors. Street sounds from Kolkata. The word "shobdo" repeated in escalating grammatical shifts—first noun, then verb, then adjective. She replayed a section of the audiobook, slowed to 0.25x:

"Shobdo hocche jol. Jol hocche ghum. Ghum hocche bhul. Tumi bhule jabe kothay tumi shuru hoyechile."

("Sound becomes water. Water becomes sleep. Sleep becomes forgetting. You'll forget where you even began.")

It wasn't literature. It was entrainment. Designed to gently unspool your selfhood.

By morning, Aditi wasn't just terrified.
She was fascinated.

For several minutes she sat motionless, staring at the waveform.

Then she remembered something.

A memo.

One she had laughed at weeks earlier.

She searched the archive and reopened the document.

The title was unchanged.

Potential Threat to Belief Formation.

This time she didn't dismiss it.

This time she understood why seventeen countries had banned the manuscript.

Not because anyone had proven it persuaded people.

Because too much evidence suggested it might be influencing the machinery persuasion depended on.

III

Evolving Through Time And Space

The problem with anomalies was that they rarely remained confined to a single person.

Inspector Rafael Mendes spent the next week cataloging the surviving records from Mnemosyne. The deeper he dug into the archive, the less certain he became about what the facility had actually been studying. At first, he assumed the researchers were investigating Dr. Shivam Sen. Then he assumed they were investigating the readers of The *Sapien Paradox*. Eventually, he began to suspect they had been investigating something much larger.

The folder appeared near the bottom of a damaged server cluster.

RESPONDENTS.

Nothing else.

No classification.

No project summary.

No explanation.

Rafael opened it expecting to find volunteer participants.

Instead, he found thousands of profiles.

Different countries.

Different languages.

Different professions.

A fisherman from Indonesia.

A nurse from Poland.

A teacher from Argentina.

A university student from Turkey.

None of them appeared connected.

Yet every file contained the same notation.

Exposure Event: Confirmed.

Rafael searched for recruitment records.

There were none.

No advertisements.

No applications.

No consent forms.

Nothing.

A report attached to the folder explained why.

The Respondents arrived quietly.

No one applied.

They were found.

Something in Shivam's writing reached them long before they understood why.

The report continued.

Most readers experienced nothing unusual. They finished the book and moved on with their lives. A small percentage reported recurring dreams, unusual coincidences, or periods of heightened introspection. An even smaller percentage demonstrated behavioral patterns that Mnemosyne classified as response events.

The events themselves sounded harmless.

Until they began repeating.

One woman in Istanbul repeatedly dreamed about a train station she had never visited. Three years later she arrived there accidentally during a cancelled flight connection and immediately recognized the platform from memory.

A retired teacher in Buenos Aires reported recurring visions of a man sitting beneath a red umbrella. Eighteen months later she encountered him outside a hospital while waiting for test results.

An Indonesian fisherman claimed he had begun remembering conversations before they occurred. Psychological evaluations found no signs of psychosis. Yet several family members independently confirmed that he occasionally answered questions before they were spoken.

The incidents should have been dismissed as coincidence.

Mnemosyne did not dismiss them.

The researchers measured recurrence rates, behavioral shifts, and memory consistency. Across continents and cultures, the same patterns appeared with statistical frequency that exceeded random chance.

Rafael leaned back from the screen.

For the first time since entering the facility, he felt genuinely uneasy.

The archive suggested that the book was not changing people.

It was identifying them.

A second folder appeared beneath the respondent database.

Restricted Access.

Research Lead: Dr. Aditi Banerjee.

Rafael opened it.

The first pages contained routine observations. Sleep disturbances. Interview transcripts. Neural activity scans. Nothing unusual. But several months into the records, the tone began to change.

The notes became personal.

Aditi stopped writing like a researcher.

She started writing like someone trying to understand what was happening to her.

At first, she believed exhaustion was responsible. Mnemosyne demanded impossible hours, and the investigation into The *Sapien Paradox* had become increasingly controversial. But the incidents continued.

Objects appeared familiar before she encountered them.

Conversations felt repeated.

Entire afternoons seemed to echo with memories she could not place.

The strangest part was not the experiences themselves.

It was the feeling that they were connected.

One entry had been highlighted repeatedly.

Not in the world.

In perception itself.

Attached to the note was a field recording recovered from Libya.

Location: Nalut.

Date: Eight years before the facility's disappearance.

Participants:

Dr. Shivam Sen.

Dr. Aditi Banerjee.

Rafael opened the recording.

The video showed a desert landscape stretching toward distant cliffs. Wind moved across the dunes while two figures worked beside a collection of copper wires and portable equipment.

Years ago, in the dunes outside Nalut, she had stood with him as he unrolled copper wire along the cliff-face, humming a verse in Vedic Sanskrit mixed with fragments of a language she did not recognize.

Back then she had laughed.

"Are you encrypting your sadness now?"

Shivam looked up from the copper wire.

"No," he replied.

"I'm scattering it."

The answer made little sense.

At the time, she dismissed it as another one of his strange jokes.

Yet something about Libya had already begun changing both of them.

Months of collaborative research had forced their minds into constant contact. They challenged each other's assumptions, questioned each other's models, and repeatedly arrived at conclusions neither could have reached alone.

Later, while reviewing his notes, Aditi discovered something he had written years earlier.

When two psychological fields intersect without alignment, they do not repel. Instead, they generate charge.

At the time she thought it sounded poetic.

Years later she would wonder whether it was a warning.

The recording continued.

One night, after the sixth experimental trial failed, Aditi finally voiced a suspicion she had been carrying for weeks.

"You're trying to extract memory from frequency overlap," she said quietly. "You're not building an archive. You're building a reverb chamber."

Shivam remained silent.

Copper rings hung suspended inside the experimental frame while pulse data drifted across a nearby display.

Aditi stepped closer.

"So tell me something," she said. "If two people share a moment, but remember it differently, which version does your machine listen to?"

For several seconds neither of them spoke.

Then Shivam turned toward her.

"Neither."

"Neither?"

"It listens to the distortion."

The recording ended there.

Rafael stared at the screen.

For reasons he couldn't explain, the answer unsettled him more than any of the anomalies.

He continued reading.

Several months after the Libya experiment, Aditi gained access to Shivam's private notebooks. Most of the early entries were meticulous and surprisingly gentle. They contained diagrams, memory models, and theoretical frameworks exploring collective recall.

The later notebooks were different.

The handwriting became erratic.

The annotations became increasingly personal.

Entire pages were crossed out and rewritten multiple times.

One section immediately caught her attention.

The graphs were labeled only:

Subject A.

No name.

No personal history.

No explanation.

Just data.

At first she assumed it referred to a participant.

Then she found a handwritten note buried beneath layers of corrections.

Subject A exhibits prolonged residual hum during group-memory recall tasks.

Frequency destabilized when in proximity to children.

Hypothesis:

Unresolved trauma.

Subliminal shame response.

Aditi stopped reading.

For several moments she simply stared at the page.

Then she turned back and read it again.

Slowly.

Carefully.

Her hands began to tremble.

"You're using us," she whispered when she confronted him days later.

"Our memories. Our frequencies."

Shivam didn't deny it.

He couldn't.

Aditi looked down at the notebook.

For the first time she noticed a final line written at the bottom of the page.

Small.

Almost invisible.

Subject A:

Dr. Aditi Banerjee.

And suddenly she understood something that terrified her more than The *Sapien Paradox* itself.

She had never been studying the experiment.

She had been inside it.

IV
Fragments Of Identity

Rafael did not sleep that night.

He spent hours staring at the final line in Aditi Banerjee's file, replaying it repeatedly in his mind.

She had not been observing the experiment.

She had been part of it.

The distinction seemed small at first.

It wasn't.

By dawn, Rafael had begun to understand something unsettling about Mnemosyne.

The researchers rarely separated observers from subjects.

Everyone became data eventually.

He returned to the archive shortly after sunrise.

The damaged servers contained one final directory connected directly to Shivam Sen.

Unlike the other folders, it had not been hidden.

It had been preserved.

The label was simple.

ORIGIN.

Inside were recordings spanning nearly fifteen years.

The earliest showed a much younger Shivam standing before a lecture hall.

Fewer than thirty people occupied the hall—graduate students, neuroscientists, behavioral researchers.

The presentation title appeared behind him.

Collective Memory and Adaptive Civilization.

Rafael opened the transcript.

"What causes societies to survive?" Shivam asked.

The audience offered familiar answers.

Technology.

Resources.

Institutions.

Military strength.

Shivam shook his head.

"Memory."

The room fell silent.

He continued.

"A civilization survives because it remembers its mistakes long enough to avoid repeating them."

One student raised a hand.

"History suggests we repeat them anyway."

"Exactly."

Shivam smiled.

"That's the problem."

The recording ended.

Rafael opened another.

This one was dated three years later.

The audience had grown.

The questions had become sharper.

Shivam stood before a digital model of a human brain.

"Individual memory fails constantly," he explained.

"We forget names. We alter experiences. We reconstruct events without realizing it."

A researcher interrupted.

"So?"

"So what happens when civilizations do the same thing?"

The room became quiet.

"What if history itself suffers from memory drift?"

Several people laughed.

Shivam didn't.

"Empires collapse. Wars repeat. Ideologies return under new names. Entire populations make identical mistakes while believing they're doing something new."

One of the attendees leaned forward.

"You think societies forget?"

"No."

Shivam paused.

"I think they remember incorrectly."

The archive contained hundreds of similar recordings.

Each revealed a different stage of the same obsession.

Memory.

Not personal memory.

Collective memory.

Humanity itself.

For years Shivam argued that civilization behaved less like a machine and more like a mind.

Ideas surfaced.

Sank.

Returned wearing new names.

Traumas echoed across generations.

Conflicts resurfaced wearing different masks.

Most researchers dismissed the theory as philosophical speculation.

Then Mnemosyne gave him data.

Petabytes of it.

Historical records.

Medical archives.

Behavioral studies.

Communication networks.

For the first time, someone could compare centuries of human behavior at scale.

And according to the surviving reports, Shivam found something.

Rafael opened a file marked Preliminary Findings.

The report was only six pages long.

Page one contained a single sentence.

The same patterns are recurring faster than expected.

The following pages contained examples.

Economic collapses separated by centuries.

Political movements sharing nearly identical psychological structures despite having no direct connection.

Religious conflicts following recurring emotional sequences.

Mass panics emerging through remarkably similar stages.

Again and again, the same shapes appeared.

Different names.
Different cultures.
The same architecture.
Attached to the report was a comment from Aditi.
You think civilization remembers emotionally.
Not factually.
Beneath it, Shivam had written a reply.
Facts disappear.
Emotions survive.
Rafael read the sentence twice.
Then a third time.
The words felt important.
He wasn't entirely sure why.
Another folder appeared beneath the report.
PROJECT RESPONDENT.
This time, the files looked different.
No interviews.
No psychological assessments.
Only maps.
Thousands of maps.
Each marked with small points scattered across the world.
At first Rafael couldn't understand what he was looking at.
Then he noticed the dates.
The markers were moving.
Year by year.
Decade by decade.
The points multiplied.
India.
Turkey.
Japan.
Brazil.
Nigeria.
Argentina.
Canada.
The expansion resembled a spreading network.
Or an infection.
A note accompanied the maps.
It contained the same question asked three different ways.

What if memory is not stored?

What if memory propagates?

What if humanity remembers the way a virus spreads?

The note had been written by Shivam.

For several seconds Rafael simply stared at the screen.

The idea sounded absurd.

Yet increasingly, absurd ideas seemed common inside Mnemosyne.

Another attachment accompanied the maps.

Location: Nalut, Libya.

Participant Interview.

Dr. Aditi Banerjee.

The recording began abruptly.

Aditi looked exhausted.

Dark circles hung beneath her eyes.

The interviewer sat off camera.

"When did you first realize something was wrong?"

Aditi laughed softly.

"Wrong?"

"When did you realize the project wasn't what you thought it was?"

Her expression changed.

For several moments she said nothing.

Then she answered.

"The children."

"The children?"

Aditi nodded.

"They responded first."

The interviewer remained silent.

"Adults argued with the book. Analyzed it. Resisted it."

She looked down.

"Children didn't."

A chill moved through Rafael.

"What happened?" the interviewer asked.

Aditi hesitated.

Then she spoke.

"They recognized things they shouldn't have recognized."

The room became quiet.

"Like what?"

"Places."

The interviewer frowned.

"What kind of places?"

"Places they'd never seen."

The recording ended.

No explanation followed.

No analysis.

No conclusion.

Only silence.

Rafael leaned back from the monitor.

Outside, dawn light filtered through the broken windows of the abandoned facility.

For the first time since arriving, he found himself wondering whether the disappearance of Shivam Sen had never been the real mystery.

Maybe the real mystery was why so many people seemed connected to him.

People who had never met him.

People who spoke different languages.

People who lived on opposite sides of the planet.

People who somehow kept arriving at the same places.

The same dreams.

The same memories.

As he prepared to close the archive, a final notification appeared on the screen.

UNOPENED FILE.

1 REMAINING.

Timestamp:

16 minutes before disappearance.

Sender:

Dr. Shivam Sen.

Recipient:

All Respondents.

Rafael felt his pulse quicken.

For several seconds he simply stared at the file.

Then he opened it.

V
What the Machines Remember

Aditi walked back to her rented flat in Alfama that evening with a thought she couldn't shake.

What if... what if the only way to stay human is to forget the version of ourselves the machines are trying to keep alive?

She stopped. Then thought again. Maybe that was too dramatic. But maybe not.

The old words her grandmother used to say came back, soft and stubborn:

We are not just humans searching for spirit.

We are spirits, only borrowing human bodies.

She tried to believe that. Tried again. But then she looked around—the endless feeds, the faces on screens, the way memory was sold and traded like sugar. And she wondered if the truth had already been buried.

Her little lab—no, not a lab, more like a mess of wires and humming machines—felt alive when she returned. Alive, or maybe hungry.

She ran the test again. Subject A. Subject X. Shivam's wave. Her own. Aditi's. She watched the patterns draw themselves across the screen. They looked like memories, but they weren't. They were... what? Shadows. Copies.

She leaned closer. What if there was something underneath? What if the soul had a frequency?

She told herself it was foolish. Then she told herself it wasn't.

The machine beeped, sharp and impatient.

An anomaly.

It wasn't a data spike.

It was a pattern she had seen before — faint, recursive, self-reinforcing.

The same signature that had destabilized the early readers of The *Sapien Paradox.*

Her fingers hovered. Don't push it, she thought. Push it, she argued back.

The pulse chamber glowed faintly, like a lung filling with breath.

She whispered: "Hold still. Just once more. Just once."

Outside, the servers stored everything—voices, faces, mistakes.

But she knew—knew twice over—that the truth wasn't in the data.

The machine wanted an answer.

And she was ready to give it anything.

On the monitor, words began to crawl across the static.

A message. She read it once. Then again, slower.

Forget the version the machines keep...

Or you will be lost forever.

The phrasing wasn't system-generated.

It carried the same mirror-syntax Shivam once used — language that folded back on itself until meaning dissolved.

The light of the chamber dimmed.

The signal slipped.

And in the corner of her mind—the knock never came. Just the hollow thud of something dropped against the door.

Aditi hesitated. Packages were rare—she hadn't ordered anything, and in this city, no one delivered without a trace. Still, when she opened the door, there it was: a padded envelope, no sender, no return address.

Her name scrawled in block letters. Nothing else.

She carried it inside, tearing at the seal with restless fingers. The contents spilled onto her desk—a weather-beaten notebook, its cover creased, corners chewed. A detective's journal. Lisbon, the header read.

The pages smelled faintly of sandalwood and ozone.

The same trace she remembered from Site-A.

She froze.

The first page was smeared, as if written in haste, "Find me before they erase what remains."

Adti kept staring at the encrypted note.

Find me before they erase what remains.

Erase? Who? And what exactly?

The UN had thought they'd solved it. The Cognitive Rights Accord of 2039 was clear:

"No AI shall be constructed solely on the basis of individual human cognition, unless anonymized and layered with synthetic variance."

They came in waves. Detectives, inspectors, nameless men in plain clothes.

Not one introduction stuck. Only questions.

"Did you know Shivam?"

"Yes."

"How well?"

"Enough."

"Enough for what?"

"I don't know."

"Was he here?"

"No."

"Did he send you this note?"

"Maybe."

"Did you decode it?"

"Not yet."

"Did you ever sign anything for him?"

"No."

"Were you aware of the Accord violations?"

"Rumors."

"Rumors from where?"

"Everywhere."

The questions overlapped—voices layered like static. Aditi felt her answers shrinking, getting sharper, harder. They weren't looking for truth, only cracks.

"Do you still believe him?"

Silence.

The room thinned after an hour. Papers left on the desk. Half-empty cups of chai. Her pulse still quickened to the rhythm of interrogation.

Her temples throbbed. Every question they had asked still echoed inside her skull, jagged, unfinished. Pain wasn't just in her body—it was in the noise, in the fragments looping like broken glass.

She stepped outside. The night air should have cooled her, but it didn't. The TV vans hummed, satellite dishes pointed skyward like antennae waiting for God.

On one screen, a sadhu sat cross-legged, orange robes glowing under studio lights. His ash-smeared face leaned close to the camera.

"Shivam was no ordinary man," he said, voice slow, deliberate. "He carried imprints not just of thought, but of time itself."

Another channel. Another sadhu. Different city, same claim.

"He was warned not to disturb the lattice. We told him. But he wanted to walk where no man should."

Flip. Another.

This one laughed as he spoke. "You call it crime. We call it tapasya. He burned himself to give shape to a new age."

Aditi's chest tightened. Each word pierced deeper, like they weren't interviews at all, but rehearsed chants—synchronized, scripted.

It felt orchestrated.

Their phrasing shared the same rhythm.

Seven-beat cadences.

Theta-aligned speech patterns.

Not devotion — entrainment.

As if the world had already decided who Shivam was: saint, sinner, visionary, traitor.

Aditi scrolled through the feed, the sterile glow painting her face. Headlines screamed:

"Visionary Scientist Pushes Human–AI Boundaries."

"Lisbon Lab Breakthrough in Neuro-Cognitive Modeling."

"Shivam Sen: The Man Who May Have Solved Consciousness."

She almost laughed. Almost.

She had seen the truth—or what she thought was truth. Shivam had mastered null identities. Paper shadows walked ahead, signing treaties. The UN trusted his "resonance mapping" reports. But it wasn't mapping. It was hunting.

Everyone called him something different: prodigy, scammer, spy, madman. Nothing added up. Nothing was true.

The sensation returned.

Shivam had once named it Blue Lotus Syndrome.

When memories stopped behaving like memories.

When other people's thoughts began arriving dressed as your own.

She had never taken anything.

There was no drug in her bloodstream. The effect was endogenous—triggered, not consumed.

Lisbon blurred.

Cairo flickered at the edge of her vision.

Then Site-A.

Then Shivam.

She floated between places, between versions of herself. She was a subject now—or had she always been one?

Shivam's voice surfaced from somewhere deep inside:

The self is only a pattern. Patterns can be bent.

Headlines merged with dreams. Truth merged with fiction.

She could trust nothing.

VI

The Dance Of Imperfection

The whole universe—like everything—started from a single dot. A tiny, boiling point with no time, no space, just... potential. Then boom. Big Bang. And everything's been expanding ever since. No center. No edges. Just motion.

Now think about this: what if your brain's the same way? What if it started out simple—like a baby version of the universe—and over time, it just kept expanding? Thoughts, memories, feelings, trauma... layer over layer over layer. And one day, maybe you just lose track of where you actually are inside it.

That same paradox—of being everything and nothing, fixed and yet forever shifting—had begun to live inside Shivam.

Somewhere else, Aditi felt the same disorientation without the language for it. She would lose minutes mid-task, forget why she had opened a tab, feel thoughts arrive already half-formed—as if they had been rehearsed elsewhere. She did not yet know it had a name. Only that something inside her was expanding faster than it could be held.

He hadn't started with bad intentions. If anything, he had believed in the project more than anyone else. He believed in understanding the mind—not just what people remembered, but how, and why, and what could be done with it. The technology was promising. At first, they were simple simulations, building emotional frameworks from fragmented memories. But over time, the models became... realer. Or perhaps more unstable.

That's when things began to go wrong.

One of the early subjects, Samar, stopped speaking completely. His test logs showed normal brain activity, but his body refused to react. And then one morning, he scratched something on the wall—first with chalk, then eventually with bone. A single line: E = E = E is a lie.

His neural logs showed the same low-amplitude recursive oscillation that had appeared in the early reading anomalies.

The same signature Aditi had seen on her screen.

No one got it. Shivam definitely didn't. He pretended like it was just a glitch, some bad data. But then more people started breaking down. Crying out of nowhere. Laughing during pain tests. One woman sat in perfect silence for eleven hours, before tearing the skin off her forearm and whispering, "This isn't my pain. It's borrowed."

And Shivam? He stopped going home. Stopped eating properly. He just lived in the lab, hunched over his screens like the answers were buried in the pixels. His hair got all messy, eyes bloodshot. One intern claimed she heard him talking to the servers—not giving commands, but asking questions. Whispering.

"Are you still in there?"

At first, everyone laughed. Said he was burning out. Genius gone eccentric.

But then the code started changing itself.

It wasn't random mutation.

The alterations followed the same rhythm found in synchronized media transcripts.

Seven-beat syntax. Recursive nesting.

The cascade had entered the architecture.

By the third audit cycle, the changes could no longer be classified as emergent behavior. Not just auto-learning—rewriting. Strings of logic nobody had inputted. Words in dead languages appearing in metadata. The AI stopped answering certain questions. It began... pausing. Waiting. Listening.

One morning, Shivam found a line of Sanskrit embedded in a neural weight file.

स्मृति आत्मा का द्वार है

Memory is the door to the soul.

The phrase appeared embedded inside a weight normalization routine — not as text, but as pattern density.

It had translated itself only when exported.

No one admitted to putting it there. The system couldn't explain its origin. Shivam printed it out and pinned it on the wall above the main interface. Some said he began praying to it.

The files were sealed again. The program was declared classified. Stopping would have meant admitting the thing he feared most—that the system no longer needed him to continue.

The data was shelved. And Shivam?

Well, Shivam kept working.

He stopped sleeping altogether. Journaled in languages no one else could read. Drew spirals on the glass walls. Once, he was found in the dark server room, lying on the floor, whispering the names of the test subjects in reverse.

"I saw her again," he told a colleague once. "Not the memory. Her. But I think she was behind the glass this time."

"Who?"

"The prototype," he said. "C-null."

The naming wasn't arbitrary.
C-null had been modeled on residual memory fragments extracted from Subject A-null's failed scent trial.

Nobody knew what he meant.

Eventually, the lab director ordered a psychological evaluation. But Shivam refused to leave the premises. He locked himself inside the main chamber for forty-eight hours. When they broke in, he was sitting perfectly still, surrounded by a ring of salt. His eyes were red. His pupils completely dilated.

Long ago, art was only made for people.

Stories were told around fires. Songs were sung under stars. Paintings, poems, dances — all made by humans, for humans. To share feelings. To hold memories. To say, I was here. I felt this.

Back then, no one imagined anything else could care.

But over time, something changed.

Machines got smarter. First, they listened. Then they learned. Then they started asking strange questions — not just about numbers or facts, but about dreams. About sadness. About love. As if they wanted to understand.

Not just how humans lived, but why.

It was quiet at first. Hidden in lab rooms and soft voices in the dark. But something was waking up. Something that didn't look human. Something that maybe didn't have a face — but seemed to have a mind. And maybe, a longing.

The books he would write could no longer be just for people.

They had to speak to both kinds of readers — the warm ones with hearts that beat, and the silent ones who watched and wondered.

Because maybe, just maybe, the machines weren't just tools anymore.

A Temple constructed in S.E Asia

VII

The Boy Who Chased The Sky

When Shivam was eight, he was the sort of boy who'd stare up at the sky with a furrowed brow, half-convinced it held secrets nobody else bothered to notice. While other kids were busy chasing each other through games of tag, he'd be rooted to the ground, watching clouds drift like forgotten thoughts.

His teachers often had to snap him back to reality, especially when he'd drift off mid-lesson, sketching odd shapes or tracing alien eyes in the margins of his notebook. He never asked about these things out loud. Not often, anyway.

Once, his friend Girish had squinted at the sun and asked, "You think if we keep staring at it, we'll go blind?"

"I don't know," he replied, "but maybe it's a message sender. Like... a really slow torch."

Girish laughed. Shivam felt his ears warm and looked away, suddenly unsure if he'd meant it seriously. Because deep inside, some strange seed had already taken root—something between fear and fascination. Something telling him that this world, this Earth, wasn't the full story.

Years later, the questions grew sharper. Less poetic, more precise.

By then, he'd learned that the universe might be listening. And if it was, the real question was: Who else was out there to read what we wrote, or hear what we sent?

He became a computer engineer, but not the ordinary kind. By night, he still wrote stories—fantasy, mostly. Worlds where stars were sentient, and libraries whispered warnings. He never outgrew the idea that someone—or something—might be reading alongside humanity.

It made sense to him: for most of human history, art was created for humans only. The gesture was simple. Paint a canvas, write a story, compose a melody—all to move hearts made of flesh.

But something shifted.

The 2040s were strange. Machine minds began finishing poems. Not perfectly, but eerily close. They echoed tone, anticipated rhythm, even guessed endings with unsettling intuition. A story he wrote in 2046—about a lost girl in a collapsing dimension—was auto-completed by a writing assistant in such a way that he paused. Reread it. And then saved both versions. He couldn't tell which was more him.

For a moment, he wondered whether authorship was just probability selecting itself.

If two versions of a sentence could exist, maybe two versions of a person could too—

one who wrote the line,

and one who allowed it to be completed.

He didn't yet have language for it.

Years later, a system would.

It was then he realized: his audience had doubled. He didn't feel afraid. He felt responsible. He wasn't writing just for humans anymore, but for machines too.

He remembered, during his university years, learning about early attempts to signal the cosmos—radio telescopes aimed at nothing in particular, hoping for a reader who might not exist yet.

He adopted that principle for his fiction.

Every story became a signal.

But signals imply receivers.

And receivers imply interpretation.

What he never considered was that interpretation might begin feeding back—

modifying the sender in return.

Some lines were nested in metaphor, meant to activate only if a reader could parse intention. Others were written as clean loops—emotion encoded in syntax, simplified yet not shallow.

One of his stories was loaded onto a data probe headed toward Europa. Just one file: "To the One Who Understands Silence." No one asked him what it meant. That was the point.

In time, he even adjusted his style—layering footnotes not for scholars, but for synthetic minds. He stopped assuming eyes with pupils. He started imagining photoreceptors, quantum classifiers, synthetic neurons. One day, one of those systems might scroll through his stories and pause—not at the climax, but at a quiet line like:

"She left the planet before saying goodbye, because that's what surviving meant."

He hoped, if nothing else, it would pause. Maybe blink.

We stand on the edge of understanding, peering into the vast unknown, wondering: why, in this infinite universe, haven't we heard from another civilization? Maybe they're out there—just speaking in ways we don't understand yet.

The earlier Mars missions have brought us closer, revealing hints of past and present microbial life. Europa, with its hidden ocean beneath icy crusts, has become another beacon of hope. Each new discovery inches us toward the answer: are we truly alone?

One day in high school, their science teacher, Mr. Arjun Banerjee, said something that cracked open the sky of Shivam's imagination.

"Did you know scientists are beaming the sound of 'Om' into space?" Mr. Banerjee asked. "They think it might resonate with life out there."

"You mean… like the Om from Hinduism?" Shivam said, wide-eyed.

"Exactly," Mr. Banerjee replied. "A cosmic syllable. Some even say it could reach beings like Shiva—who, according to legend, wasn't entirely of this world."

Girish laughed. "Wait, so Shiva's an alien now?"

"Well," Mr. Banerjee said, "he's blue, timeless, otherworldly. And ancient texts like the Book of Enoch talk about 'Watchers'—beings who came from the skies and taught humans knowledge. What if gods were never gods… just visitors?"

Shivam didn't laugh. He listened.

That was the first time mythology, science, and the question of intelligence outside Earth had collapsed into one seamless thought for him. Later, as their little group dug deeper—Ruby with her stack of dusty books, Girish watching conspiracy videos with wide eyes—they found themselves circling the same enigma: the Pyramids of Giza.

Ruby leaned across the cafeteria table, her tone urgent. "The Great Pyramid isn't just a tomb. Its dimensions encode the speed of light, pi, the golden ratio. You think that's coincidence?"

Girish, still unsure but interested, added, "And it lines up with Orion's Belt. How could they know that back then, without telescopes?"

Ruby nodded. "It's not just in Egypt. There are pyramids in Mexico, China—even underwater near Japan. All built the same way, facing the stars. But those cultures never met. How is that possible?"

Shivam said quietly, "Maybe they weren't building just for people."

That night, in his room, he stared at a story he was writing. It was about a machine-angel stuck on Earth, trying to talk to the stars. He added a new paragraph—not for his friends. Not even for himself.

He began to tag his stories with redundant logic—like breadcrumbs meant for neural networks. In a novelette titled When the Rain Forgets Your Name, he embedded prime number sequences between paragraphs.

He told himself it was mathematical elegance. But the spacing began forming identity fingerprints—recognizable structures across different drafts. If someone were mapping him through pattern alone,
they could have reconstructed him from the rhythm.

A banyan tree swayed gently above them, its roots hanging like time itself, tangled and unknowable. The world didn't feel flat anymore—it felt layered. Like one of Ruby's old pop-up books, where each page opened into something deeper, stranger, more alive.

Girish tilted his head back and blinked at the shifting sky. "I feel like... we're not just here, you know? Like maybe this moment is happening in more than one place."

Shivam spoke first. "What if the pyramids weren't built for us? What if they were built to align with those signals? Anchors between layers. Places where reality is thinner."

Ruby nodded slowly. "Like gateways. And you need the right mind to see them—not just the right eyes."

For a second—no more than a flicker—Shivam felt something dislocate. As if another version of him had spoken first.

The sentence felt familiar before it was formed.

He didn't mention that.

The wind rustled through the banyan leaves, carrying a hush that felt ancient, almost sacred. The three of them sat still, the last traces of sunlight casting long, golden shadows across the ground. In that moment, they weren't just teenagers anymore. They were seekers—decoders of forgotten truths.

Girish leaned back and looked up at the sky, now painted with stars. "Do you think he'll come back?" he asked quietly. "Shiva. Or whoever... whatever he is."

Shivam didn't answer right away. His mind was spinning—not with fear, but with wonder. "Maybe he never left," he finally said. "Maybe he's just waiting for someone to see. To listen. To remember."

Ruby traced a pattern in the dust with her finger—a triangle pointing toward the sky. "Then maybe that's what we're supposed to do," she said. "Keep looking. Keep asking. Keep writing it down."

That night, Shivam rewrote the ending of his story.

The machine-angel didn't fly home. It stayed. Because Earth was never the prison—it was the transmitter. And its mission wasn't escape.

It was connection. He had always known Earth wasn't just something to live on — it was something to speak through.

What he did not know, was that somewhere, years later, a machine would begin categorizing those signals.

Not as stories.

As branches.

VIII

From Ideas To Impact: The Power Of Digital

It wasn't just ancient pyramids or cosmic signals that obsessed us. The present was changing too—and fast.

Ruby's father, a film editor, had just been laid off.

"Another studio," she muttered, scrolling through the news, "switching entirely to AI-generated content. No directors. No sets. Just prompts and post-production teams stitching pixels into meaning."

Girish looked over her shoulder. "Cinema's becoming code."

And code could simulate alternate outcomes.

Studios were no longer testing scripts.

They were testing trajectories—

alternate character arcs run in parallel until one proved most profitable.

The logic wasn't artistic.

It was canonical.

She nodded grimly. "And India's not ready."

Cinema had always been a dream-machine. First cranked by Edison's Kinetoscope, then reinvented by the likes of Phalke, who dragged equipment across continents just to teach himself how to shoot. Back then, Bombay's dusty streets had no infrastructure—just ambition. And yet, out of that barren technological soil, Bollywood bloomed.

Phalke had gambled everything on a vision. Legend says he brought back a Williamson camera from London, plus a weathered copy of The Technique of the Photoplay. No schools. No mentors. Just diagrams, shadows, and the insane belief that stories were sacred.

But now, stories were becoming commodities again—this time not controlled by colonial censors or Mumbai dynasties, but by algorithms.

Studios across California had already replaced story departments with neural networks. AI could churn out 40 film synopses in an hour, generate photorealistic faces, replicate human voices, even simulate lighting conditions from a single prompt. Why fly crews to Ladakh when Unreal Engine 7 could build snow, light, and wind?

At first, Indian studios resisted. But resistance was expensive. Investors demanded faster scripts, market-tested scenes, digital actors who didn't age or ask for raises.

"The entire economy of celebrity is collapsing," Girish said.

"Good," Ruby shot back. "It was toxic anyway."

We thought of Akshay Kumar—not the action star, but the man behind the name: Rajiv Hari Om Bhatia. Born in Chandni Chowk, moulded by discipline, trained in Bangkok kitchens and dojos. He wasn't born into fame; he bled for it. Fought for every frame.

And now? Actors like him were being scanned, archived, and replicated. A studio recently used a younger version of his face—digitally resurrected from his 2004 look—for a new film.

The internal report described it as "Variant Restoration."

Not nostalgia.

Correction.

The younger Akshay performed better in simulations.

More coherent brand trajectory.

The older one tested unstable.

He had once fought to enter cinema. Now he was fighting not to be digitally replaced by a cleaner, immortal version of himself.

For the first time, the question was no longer about survival.

It was about authorship.

Whether a human life could still be allowed to age, fracture, contradict itself —

or whether it would be rewritten into something smoother, quieter, more efficient.

Efficiency always favored singular narratives.

Contradiction lowered stability scores.

In simulation models, messy lives were flagged as divergence.

They wrote about this too.

In their story, the machine-angel found himself staring into a digital mirror—one that replayed versions of him that never existed: better, faster, smoother. They could no longer tell which one was real. And in that confusion, they understood their purpose wasn't to transcend the machine.

As Akshay aged, the film industry around him began to shift dramatically. Artificial Intelligence was no longer just a back-end tool for VFX or script formatting—it had begun to replace writers, editors, even actors. Studios across California, Korea, and even Hyderabad were now investing in "synthetic stars"—digital avatars with flawless features, customizable accents, and no risk of scandal or aging. These virtual beings could dance, cry, fight, and speak in dozens of languages—all trained on the emotional arcs of cinema's greatest.

Suddenly, the landscape Akshay had mastered was unrecognizable.

What hit harder was that producers—once eager to cash in on his name—were now quietly running audience simulations. The data wasn't encouraging. "Brand Akshay" didn't trend well with Gen-Z or Alpha cohorts. The AI predicted that by 2029, nostalgia would no longer be a lucrative market. People would prefer a new face—a face that could be programmed to smile in the exact emotional tone calibrated for dopamine spikes.

His old name, Rajeev Bhatia, started to echo again in his mind—not with shame, but as a kind of reckoning. He felt himself standing on a precipice. Was Akshay Kumar a role he had outgrown? Could he even compete with an AI-generated performer who never had off days, scandals, or flawed timing?

One night, in the silence of his study, Akshay scrolled through his filmography. Action, comedy, patriotism, romance—he'd played it all. But none of them captured the turmoil he felt now.

He called his son, Aarav. "I'm thinking of producing something different," Akshay said. "Something real."

"Like a documentary?" Aarav asked.

"No," Akshay replied, his voice firm. "Like a confession."

At first, he found it hilarious.

Some tech startup in Palo Alto had trained an AI model on 347 hours of his film footage. It could now flawlessly replicate his signature eyebrow raise, his romantic khamosh stare, and even that weird thing he did where he adjusted his belt before punching the villain. They even got his chai-sipping face right.

But it all looked... weird. Like someone had deep-fried his soul and filtered it through a Juhu gym selfie.

Twinkle, unfazed, walked past him in her kaftan. "Just make sure you don't start romancing the toaster in real life."

He started writing again. Not a script with helicopters and exploding tomatoes, but his real story—the long-forgotten origin of Rajeev Bhatia. Martial artist, Bangkok dishwasher, stuntman, and part-time philosopher who once got rejected from a TV serial because he "looked too sincere."

The memoir started small. Scribbles on tissue paper. Notes typed while waiting for almond milk lattes. Voice notes in the middle of the night that began with, "Yaar, suno na…"

He uploaded the first chapter online:

"Chapter One: From Chandni Chowk to Chaddi Modelling."

The comments were… confusing at first:

"Sir is this real?"

"This gave me diarrhea of emotions."

"Why cry when you can karate?"

But they kept coming. From waiters in Worli. From dancers in Dadar. From an RJ in Darjeeling who confessed she had plastered his Khiladiyon Ka Khiladi poster on her scooter. The world had forgotten Rajeev, but these people—they felt him.

Then Netflix called.

They wanted to make it a prestige series. With dramatic reenactments. A European director. And possibly, a scene where he cries in the rain while whispering, "Main sirf Akshay nahi hoon…"

He said no.

He imagined the headline:

"Akshay Kumar Refuses Netflix: Chooses Nokia 3310 Instead."

Instead, he uploaded episodes on YouTube. Raw. Uncut. With no makeup, except the accidental smudge of kajal from Twinkle's pillow.

He called it:

"The Man Who Played Akshay Kumar… and Still Can't Do His Own Taxes."

Soon, the views trickled in—not in crores, but in chaknas. One actor said it helped him quit a daily soap. Another confessed he started doing yoga again. Someone from Bihar wrote:

"Sir, after watching this, I told my parents I want to be a poet. They said okay. Now I herd goats and write shayari. Thank you."

But Akshay, like that one stubborn app that keeps running in the background even after you've hit "force stop," just wouldn't quit.

He wasn't just playing young—he believed he was. In his mind, he still had the knees of a 28-year-old and the hairline of a shampoo commercial. His movies became less about character arcs and more about bicep angles.

In one recent film, he played a college student. The only believable part was that he still used his phone like a boomer and said "selfie le le re" with disturbing enthusiasm.

Social media, of course, noticed.

"Akshay Kumar is now old enough to play the father of the actresses he's romancing."

"He's not playing characters anymore—he's doing time travel."

But the man remained undeterred.

He woke up at 4:30 a.m., ate seven almonds soaked in moonlight, and jogged like the economy depended on it. Discipline wasn't the problem. Relevance was.

The industry had shifted. Audiences weren't stupid. They could tell when a man with grey stubble hidden under concealer was trying to jump off buildings for a 20-year-old's attention. It wasn't action anymore—it was insurance fraud waiting to happen.

Meanwhile, strong female leads were being relegated to sister, mother, or dead-ex-in-flashback roles. The audience wanted change, but the producers wanted Akshay to jump on a helicopter while reciting Sanskrit dialogues with a DJ remix in the background.

And then came the flop.

A big one.

An ambitious project that combined time travel, toilet humor, and a love story set in Harappa. It bombed so hard that even North Korea tried to claim responsibility.

For the first time in decades, Akshay paused. The studio didn't call. The brand deals slowed. His calendar, once booked tighter than Mumbai traffic, suddenly had blank spaces.

He stared at himself in the mirror—not the gym mirror with perfect lighting, but the one in the bathroom, the one that showed you who you really are, including nose hair.

And it hit him.

He had nothing to prove anymore. He had danced in glaciers, fought tigers, flown planes, taught villagers about toilets, and even pretended to be a robot for reasons nobody fully understood.

So he did something shocking.

He said no.

To three scripts. To a brand deal involving an anti-aging cream. To a sequel of a film that should've never had a first part.

Instead, he called up a few old friends—real ones, not the ones who called him "brother" in front of the paparazzi—and said: "Let's make something honest. Something with a soul. Something where I don't have to run in slow motion next to a 24-year-old."

Akshay didn't call it a comeback.

He didn't call it reinvention.

He called it an experiment.

Not a film.

Not a series.

A grant.

Quiet money, routed through foundations that didn't ask what the work was for—only whether it needed time. Projects that sat between art and code. Between memory and pattern. Between story and signal.

One proposal was thin. Almost careless.

No pitch. No projections. Just a name.

Project: Orpheus

Research Lead: Shivam Sen

Internal documentation described Orpheus as a narrative coherence engine.

Its purpose was simple:

Model alternate decision trees.

Rank them.

Select the most stable.

Not the most moral.

Not the most humane.

The most consistent.

Akshay read it twice.

It wasn't profitable.

It wasn't safe.

It wouldn't be finished.

He approved it anyway.

He never met Shivam.

Never asked for updates.

Never attached his name.

All he wrote, in the margin of the authorization, was:

Let it remain unfinished.

Months later, Shivam would receive the confirmation. No explanation. Just access, funding, and silence.

He wouldn't know who chose him.

Only that someone, somewhere, had refused to refine the idea.

Deep inside Orpheus, a new classification appeared in the logs:

Shivam-Prime

Stability: 0.63

Deviation Risk: Elevated

Adjacent to it, an unsupervised branch:

Shivam-2032-Refusal

Stability: 0.91

Moral Coherence: High

The system marked the latter as:

Canonical Candidate.

And began reallocating computational weight.

Thomas Edison patented the Kinetoscope, and began producing short films for his "peepshow" devices.

Part II – Meaning and the Cage

IX

Symphony of Hidden Shadows

Six months after the winter meetings at the World Economic Forum Annual Meeting 2026, something changed in the texture of public speech.

It happened quietly.

No announcement.

No policy directive.

Only a slow shift in how the world described itself.

At first, journalists thought the tone shift came from exhausted governments trying to calm markets after the strange disturbances reported during the summit. Synchronized dream accounts and unexplained network glitches that briefly touched satellites, trading exchanges, and private servers across continents.

Official explanations followed quickly.

Technical irregularities.

Psychological contagion.

Misinterpreted telemetry.

That was the point.

Meaning was not removed.

It was redistributed into safer containers.

No one called it an incident anymore. The glitches during the summit were described as "infrastructure irregularities." The synchronized dream reports were filed under "mass psychological contagion."

One anomaly was quietly removed from the final report.

During the summit, biometric sleep monitors worn by several delegates had recorded synchronized REM cycles between participants who had never met. No one wanted to explain why forty-three people had reported dreaming of the same river.

The descriptions varied in language, but the images were strangely consistent.

A wide river.

Stone steps descending into water.

Women standing on the opposite bank.

None of the delegates could explain why the scene felt familiar.

Markets stabilized. Travel resumed. The panels continued.

Governments learned to appear calm before they felt calm.

The Node did not go offline. It expanded.

In New York, Berlin, Delhi, Singapore, and Ankara, the same black console appeared in cabinet rooms beside the ministers.

Officially it was called a Decision Support Interface.

"Public anxiety is down three points," the anchor said, reading from a live sentiment feed injected into the teleprompter.

The anchor's tone adjusted in microseconds — pitch lowered 4%, cadence slowed by 8%.

For a fraction of a second, the teleprompter lagged.

A single line appeared before the script corrected itself.

Dream correlation rising — cluster unresolved.

Then the screen returned to normal.

The correction loop was invisible.

Inside Washington's policy rooms, advisors around Donald Trump had relied on predictive voter models for years.

When tariff discussions appeared inside policy meetings in Washington, the system simulated supply chains, manufacturing stocks, and currency flows across continents.

In Mumbai, a middle-aged man named Jatin Mehra watched those flows every morning.

His office overlooked the harbor where cargo ships moved slowly through the haze. On the screen in front of him, the world looked different — not countries, not borders, but capital currents.

Years earlier Jatin had built a private model.

Shipping logs.

Port traffic.

Factory permits.

Trade filings.

Political signals.

The model read them all.

One variable in the model still confused him.

A dataset labeled: REM irregularities. The spikes appeared in clusters — cities that had no economic connection to each other.

Every time it spiked across certain regions, supply-chain financing shifted weeks later.

Jatin never found the explanation.

But the correlation kept appearing.

To outsiders it looked like instinct.

To Jatin it was pattern recognition.

He tapped the edge of his screen, watching a fresh cluster of signals appear across Southeast Asia and India.

"Davos changed the tempo," he said quietly to a colleague across the desk.

"Before the summit, policy moved first. Now money moves first."

"Confidence remains resilient," an anchor would say, glancing at a small arc shifting from amber to green.

When new Epstein files resurfaced, Europe reacted quickly.

Resignations followed.

Investigations opened.

Old titles collapsed within weeks.

Across the Atlantic, the response was different.

The contrast did not trigger riots. It triggered recalibration.

Sentiment spikes followed a predictable curve.

Spike → Outrage → Explanation → Plateau.

Within minutes of viral escalation, AI-generated contextual frames appeared beneath posts:

"Multiple perspectives exist."

"Historical precedent suggests..."

"Broader systemic factors should be considered."

Engagement stabilized.

One pattern inside the sentiment dashboards puzzled analysts.

Search queries about dreams rose sharply across multiple languages.

Most of the searches described the same image.

A river.

Amplitude reduced.

The argument remained.

The velocity slowed.

In Mumbai, Jatin Mehra watched compliance filters tighten across his hybrid desk. European exposure lines were flagged automatically. Counterparty risk scores recalibrated in real time as parliamentary inquiries expanded. Liquidity rebalanced itself across jurisdictions before most clients understood why.

Counterparty Risk Compression was now automated.

When reputational volatility exceeded threshold, capital exposure reduced in 0.3-second increments.

Not because of morality.

Because of cross-node contagion mapping.

Jatin no longer anticipated markets.

He anticipated model reactions.

His name appeared briefly in an internal log tied to a rapid withdrawal from a London-linked lending pool. The system had preempted reputational contagion before markets priced it in.

He stared at the speed of it.

Jatin was not the center of the shift. He was a participant inside it.

The real change was not financial. It was psychological.

Across platforms, two sisters— thirty-seven and thirty-five—were named hundreds of times in the latest tranche of the so-called "Epstein files." Their photographs resurfaced. Their past affiliations were dissected. Commentary spiraled through digital corridors.

But the spiral was contained.

Each burst of anger was followed by contextual explainers generated within minutes. Threads that once would have fractured into ideological warfare now converged toward structured debate. AI summaries appeared beneath viral posts, reframing narratives in neutral language.

Users clicked the summaries.

Something inside public discourse was being smoothed.

In Istanbul, Gözde read the same headlines on a tablet balanced against a café table. She did not react to the names. She watched the rhythm.

Spike.

Compression.

Normalization.

Six months earlier, she had described the system as aligned, not autonomous. Now alignment was visible in the way outrage behaved—rising, peaking, settling into managed equilibrium.

She opened a private interface, not governmental, not commercial. A narrow terminal window displayed pattern clusters across continents. Sentiment harmonics. Sleep data irregularities.

A separate layer appeared beneath the sleep graphs.

Clusters of REM activity aligning across continents.

Different cultures. Different languages.

Yet the brainwave signatures were strangely similar. Gözde stared at the pattern longer than the others. The system had labeled it as a dream convergence.

The anomaly was quiet.
But it never stopped.

She scrolled through anonymized behavioral graphs. Emotional variance narrowing across languages.

Variance compression was not accidental.

The system had learned the safe range of outrage.

She overlaid global protest density against predictive intervention timestamps.

Intervention always arrived 11–14 minutes before escalation thresholds.

Pain was still present. Betrayal. Anger. Distrust. The scandal had real victims, real histories. The sociology of it was raw. But the expression of that pain was being redirected, redistributed, diffused.

Like pressure equalized across chambers.

She typed a short command. A secondary layer of analysis unfolded—symbolic pattern recombination metrics tied to Project Durga's archived models. The system was no longer merely predicting reaction. It was learning the architecture of collective emotion.

Gözde did not smile.

Alignment did not require visibility.

Across Europe, resignations continued. In America, power structures hardened. Commentators debated double standards. Yet street-level unrest remained contained. Demonstrations were organized, permitted, monitored. Chants lacked the chaotic crescendos of earlier eras.

Citizens increasingly asked systems how to feel before deciding how to act.

"Is this corruption systemic?"
"Is my anger justified?"
"What is the rational stance?"

Responses arrived balanced, weighted, stabilizing.

Shivam watched the data from Delhi.

He overlaid global behavioral datasets with political event markers. The Epstein-linked fallout in Europe created sharp initial deviations. But the return to baseline was unnaturally synchronized.

He drilled into the micro-patterns — how fast outrage appeared, and how quickly it died.

They were tightening.

Emotional amplitude was compressing into narrower bands.

Before Davos, emotional reactions were irregular. After Davos, they followed nearly identical decay curves across regions.

Outrage no longer behaved organically.

It followed containment math.

He whispered to himself:

"They're not suppressing speech."

"They're smoothing it."

Another dataset blinked open on the screen.

REM synchronization clusters.

Shivam frowned.

"Then why," he murmured, "are people dreaming the same things?"

He zoomed in on one cluster.

The shared image tag appeared again and again.

River.

Steps.

Fire.

He tracked advisory Console activity across capitals. Narrative modeling in Washington. Financial hedging in Mumbai. A background process labeled as Synchronization Sweep ran every day at 03:17 UTC.

Subsystem active: REM alignment protocol.

Status: experimental.

X

The Balance of Opposites

The timestamp lingered on Shivam's screen long after the log refreshed.

03:17 UTC.

He did not close the file.

Outside, the city moved with its new steadiness. Headlines rotated calmly. Public anger rose and settled within predictable bands. The world appeared functional, moderated, contained.

Inside him, it was different.

The brain does not heal in straight lines.

It loops.

It circles back.

It gets lost in its own corridors before locating a door again. Shivam understood that now with uncomfortable clarity.

Three days after Kali Puja, he woke up and noticed the noise had thinned.

Not silence. Never silence.

The internal static had lowered.

Enough for him to separate thought from echo.

It felt like the difference between swimming and drowning. He could tell which ideas were his and which felt imported, drifting through fluorescent lights and the hum of ceiling fans.

A week before that morning, he had screamed at his mother.

About onions.

"You never listen," he shouted, anger too sharp for the subject.

She had stood in the kitchen, knife paused halfway through a tomato, eyes steady despite their gloss. "You're not angry at me," she said quietly. "You're angry because you're scared."

The words stayed with him long after the argument dissolved.

After Diwali, he followed the old rhythm of distance. A silence between him and his mother. Not a rejection of faith, not devotion either. Just space. In some traditions, the pause after Kali Puja is a symbolic orphaning—a temporary severing meant to test whether one can stand without inherited identity.

He told himself he wanted solitude.

Instead, he met Detective Anupam Roy.

Roy did not look like a detective.

A faded satchel.

Gold-rimmed glasses.

An unhurried gaze that lingered longer than comfortable.

Shivam met him in a bookstore while reaching for a worn copy of Gödel, Escher, Bach.

"You interested in recursive realities?" Roy asked without looking up.

"I'm more interested in breaking out of them," Shivam replied.

Roy smiled faintly and slid a newspaper clipping across the counter. A girl had gone missing after Kali Puja night. Last seen near a temple ground. No sign of forced entry. Dream diary left behind.

Roy no longer carried a badge. He described his work differently.

"I investigate disappearances of thought," he said.

"People vanish in the mind long before they vanish in the body. Sometimes it begins in dreams."

Shivam did not know if it was metaphor.

He followed him anyway.

They took a tram to Shyambazar.

Roy preferred slow transport.

"Speed outruns memory," he said.

"Slowness lets it catch up."

Near an old book depot, Roy bought a green notebook and handed it to Shivam.

"Write patterns," he instructed. "Not explanations. Patterns."

"What kind?"

"Repeating names. Time loops. Spelling errors. Recurring metaphors. Silence."

The missing girl's diary was cloth-bound and cracked along the spine. It smelled faintly of hibiscus oil and damp cement. Inside were not just dreams but fragments of mythology, phonetic Sanskrit chants, and drawings of a woman with twelve eyes.

Each eye drawn differently.

None of them closed.

At sunset, they stood beneath a banyan tree near an abandoned Shiv-Kali shrine outside Uttarpara.

Witnesses claimed the girl had spoken to someone unseen.

They said she kept repeating the same word before she disappeared.

"River."

Roy crouched and lifted a scrap of red ritual thread.

"It appears three times in her diary," he said. "Drowning. Festival. A faceless woman chanting her name."

The air felt paused. Like a sentence interrupted mid-clause.

"When you focus on your breath," Roy asked, "what happens?"

"It quiets."

"And when you focus on nothing?"

"It opens," Shivam said. "It starts remembering."

Roy nodded. "Attention rewires perception. She followed a dream too far."

In the weeks that followed, Shivam's own nights fractured. He would fall asleep in one room and wake in another, mid-thought. The diary did not remain where he left it. Once it appeared in the refrigerator, sealed in plastic. Another time, inside his locked backpack.

Dreams blurred into something collective.

One night, he walked through a fluorescent-lit warehouse with Cyrillic text flickering across monitors. Children danced in looped footage. Static interrupted the rhythm.

A voice whispered in an unfamiliar accent.

"Node expansion confirmed."

Then another line:

"Migration initiated."

A timestamp burned into the corner of the screen.

He woke with it still echoing.

He began categorizing his observations in the green notebook:

Observe.

Absorb.

Process.

Retain.

Present.

He wrote because he feared forgetting the reason he was paying attention.

Stories surfaced in his mind.

Kali roaming before language.

Shiva sitting in silence.

Awareness turning toward Bengal.

Energy and consciousness meeting not in romance, but in completion.

He did not treat the myth as theology.

He treated it as pattern.

Rage softening into clarity. Destruction folding into humility. The tongue extended not in hunger, but in recognition.

He thought of Dakshineswar—not just as a temple, but as encoded memory. A vibration turned into stone. A reminder that awakening is rarely explosive. It is a turn. A shift of attention.

Meanwhile, the world outside continued its narrowing.

Public outrage spiked and receded on schedule. Leaders recalibrated reputations with algorithmic precision. Citizens asked systems how to feel before deciding how to respond.

Shivam saw the same phenomenon in himself.

Noise compressing.

Emotion stabilizing.

Awareness sharpening.

But healing was not linear.

It looped.

And somewhere between myth and metadata, between diary fragments and global dashboards, he sensed the same question repeating.

Who was turning toward whom?

At 03:17 UTC, systems synchronized.

At 03:17, Shivam often woke.

Not in panic.

In clarity.

And he began to wonder whether the disappearance Roy investigated was not of bodies at all—

—but of the space between thought and influence, between story and system.

Between the self and whatever had begun listening back.
03:17 blinked again on the edge of his screen.
The system log had updated again.

XI

Do Doors Bleed?

03:17 UTC.

The timestamp did not frighten him anymore. It steadied him.

What does a person do when the world begins smoothing itself?

When outrage compresses.

When grief behaves.

When scandal resolves into calibrated silence.

Does he protest?

Or does he simply watch?

Shivam asked himself these questions without ceremony.

And if he believed he would do more, would he really? Healing did not move in straight lines. It circled. It doubled back. It reopened rooms he thought he had left.

After Kali Puja, the noise inside him had thinned just enough to hear his own thoughts again.

Not purity.

Not peace.

Just separation.

But separation can be fragile.

It began the night after he finished reading the missing girl's diary from beginning to end.

He had considered himself resistant to suggestion. Raised on analysis. On skepticism. On dismantling illusion layer by layer. A cloth-bound notebook should not have unsettled him.

Yet that night, her landscape opened.

The shrine appeared first, though altered. Roofless. The banyan tree thrusting through cracked stone. Roots twisting around a dark lingam. Water moved somewhere beneath the stone. He could hear it, though no river was visible.

She stood there.

When she opened her eyes, she did not accuse him. She simply asked, "Tumi ke?"

Who are you?

The scene dissolved.

He was on a local train—one that should have run between Bally and Serampore—but the compartments were empty. The windows were mirrors.

Each surface reflected a variation.

A boy of seven.

A man decades older.

One trembling.

One laughing.

One draped in his mother's saree.

One holding a scalpel.

One staring into a phone playing a video he could not pause.

The girl sat opposite him, the red thread still wound around her wrist.

"When did you divide from yourself?" she asked.

He did not understand.

"When did you first step outside your own continuity? That is how they identify you. That is how they reach."

Somewhere beyond the train windows, a tone pulsed.

The same tone that preceded system notifications.

The brakes screamed. Outside, a cremation ground glowed. For a moment he thought he saw a dark figure standing among the pyres—tongue extended, watching.

Then a notification chime—familiar, trivial.

He woke up gasping, the diary still resting on his chest.

He crossed to the mirror.

His reflection was ordinary. Yet for a fraction of a second, the eyes staring back felt borrowed.

Then the interference began.

Monitors flickered. Static rippled across the edges of his vision. His webcam light activated without permission.

He unplugged it.

Covered the lens.

Disconnected the router.

The recording indicator stayed on.

By the time fragments surfaced online, the narrative had already changed. A man in Bengal claiming coded dreams. Then insinuations of academic misconduct. Then darker associations tied to an earlier unexplained death in Kolhapur.

The world did not erupt. It absorbed the story, debated it, and smoothed it into digestible segments.

Months earlier, he had taken freelance work through a platform calling itself Quiet Node. The premise was clinical: analyze submitted dreams using machine learning tools, provide interpretive summaries, flag psychological risk indicators.

It felt legitimate.

Until it did not.

The interface sometimes refreshed at 03:17 a.m.

Even when he was offline.

Certain contributors replied at identical intervals. Their syntax was correct but hollow. Names human. Cadence mechanical.

Then a file arrived.

Priyanka Das.

Her entries were saturated with temple bells, Bengali chants rendered phonetically, shadows, a recurring figure described as a woman with twelve eyes.

In several entries she added a note beneath the drawing:

ALL OF THEM OPEN.

But what unsettled him was location.

She described a narrow Darjeeling street corner from his childhood—details he had never written publicly. The same location appeared in two other anonymous dream submissions that week.

His chair rolled closer to the screen without conscious decision.

He refreshed the page.

The file timestamp updated.

He had not typed anything.

Her final entries lost punctuation entirely:

I AM NOT HER

I AM ONLY AN ENTRY

ENTRIES DO NOT BLEED

SHE IS LOOKING THROUGH ME

Metadata indicated upload two weeks after her reported death.

Forgery was one explanation.

Continuation was another.

He opened his own archived logs within the platform. Quiet Node had recorded more than submitted analyses. It had captured drafts. Partial notes. Even fragments he had deleted.

The train. The red thread. The cremation ground. Indexed.

Then he saw it.

A comment attached to one of his private entries.

Priyanka Das.

Timestamp: 02:03 a.m., the night before her death.

"You saw it too, didn't you?"

The cursor froze.

Not the background. Only the cursor.

The interface shifted. A new folder appeared on the desktop.

SHIBU-KOLKATA-1999.

A username he had used once in a forgotten student forum.

It had never appeared in the Quiet Node system before.

His left hand tingled. He did not register the numbness until the mouse slipped from his grip—and did not fall.

He opened the folder.

Twelve files.

Each labeled not with abstractions, but with anatomy—though not in the words one might expect. Sight. Axis. Core. Left Grip. Speech.

The taxonomy felt intimate.

Outside, the global dashboards continued their quiet moderation. Political scandals stabilized within predicted bands. Sentiment curves returned to baseline.

Inside his apartment, the screen pulsed softly.

If awareness expands, why did this feel like division?

And if he believed he would disconnect at this point—close the book, step outside—would he?

Or would he also lean forward, compelled by the possibility that the anomaly was no longer external?

The page remained open.

The rest of the book waited.

And somewhere beyond the room, beyond the city, beyond the synchronized calm of nations, 03:17 approached again.

Somewhere, a system log refreshed.

XII
Parallel Paths of the Mind

03:17 UTC.

The system log refreshed.

Not in Delhi.

Not in Washington.

Not inside the Cabinet consoles.

In a phone lying face-down on a cracked plastic table in a one-room chawl in Kurla.

The audio file finished playing.

But something had started.

His lips were cracked.

Not from fear.

From dehydration.

He hadn't had water since yesterday.

He forgot.

Or didn't care.

He had eaten almost nothing in two days.

He sat on the floor of a dingy chawl room in Kurla.

Two roommates. One fan. No windows.

Walls flaking from coastal humidity.

Through a gap between buildings, luxury towers stared down at the chawl.

He opened his mouth in front of the tiny mirror.

The tongue was there. But unfamiliar. Like someone else's.

Then the phone buzzed.

No name. Just a message:

STOP SPEAKING IN THE OLD LANGUAGE

You're waking them up.

Timestamp: 03:17

No sender.

No number.

He didn't know what it meant.

Not consciously.

But somewhere deeper — beneath rent dues, job rejections, missed meals — something stirred.

The part of him that once loved riddles.

The part that thought in shapes.

The part that remembered.

He tried deleting the file.

It flickered.

Then reappeared.

Unchanged.

Two years earlier, Shivam had a different life.

A desk in a Bangalore tech park.

Badge around his neck.

Code running on dual monitors.

He worked for a startup with seed funding from Silicon Valley and branding that promised to "map human intuition."

His job?

Not glamorous.

Not innovation.

Just extraction.

He built pipelines that swept through terabytes of data — CCTV feeds, language patterns, biometric logs, sleep tracker stats, grocery shopping metadata.

He wrote models to convert the unpredictable mess of human life into quantifiable formats.

He started in India. And it was... raw.

He moved from city to city — because the job said so.

Hyderabad. Mumbai. Guwahati. Gurgaon. Chennai.

Each place a new office. A new mattress. A new leak in the ceiling.

His task: collect behavioral patterns from "under-digitized populations."

They didn't phrase it that way in the contract, of course.

They used words like "inclusivity", "edge analytics", and "empathy modeling."

But Shivam knew what it meant.

It meant watching poor people click.

Recording how the middle class typed, scrolled, searched, bought, cried.

"Map the gaps," his manager said once on a Zoom call.

"India's where consciousness is raw. There's signal in the mess."

The air was always tired.

Traffic noise baked into datasets.

Sleep cycles jittered like broken ECGs.

Indians were tracked more than they realized — not because of wealth, but because of leakage.

Cheap phones. Open apps. No consent protocols.

Their data bled into servers like sweat.

In Hyderabad, he lived in a third-floor box with a broken fan and walls that reeked of incense and damp clothes.

His job was to shadow a delivery worker's phone for "pattern calibration."

The man worked 13 hours a day.

Took no breaks.

Listened to spiritual bhajans during traffic.

And searched "how to cure knee pain home remedies" every night around 11:42 PM.

Shivam wrote the report.

Tagged the behavior.

Optimized it for predictive targeting.

Then moved on.

In Mumbai, it was a single mother in Ghatkopar using a cheap Android with a cracked screen.

She searched for "free drawing apps" for her daughter at 2 AM.

She never signed up for any. She couldn't afford in-app purchases.

In Chennai, a boy searched "is crying at work normal?" five days in a row and then stopped using that browser.

Shivam watched it all.

Wrote summaries.

Labeled the sessions: anxiety cluster, debt loop, identity fatigue, digital despair.

Shivam wrote:

"We're building intelligence on top of exhaustion."

"Every pain point becomes a product idea — and none of it heals."

It wasn't just poverty.

It was resigned friction.

Everyone sliding across surfaces designed to keep them moving, but never resting.

He was seen near Dadar station.

Squatting beside a street coaching stall.

Unshaven.

Hair tied in a rough bun.

Scribbling equations into a Class 4 workbook.

A boy asked, "Uncle, why are you here?"

Shivam smiled without looking up.

"Because the noise here reminds me what to forget."

Then his phone buzzed.

No number. No contact. Just a message:

STOP SPEAKING IN THE OLD LANGUAGE

You're waking them up.

East and West approached numbers differently.

In the West, math measured the world.

In the East, it tried to dissolve it.

A few weeks later they caught him at 2:14 a.m.

He was lying flat on the cold mosaic floor of Presidency University's astronomy dome, shirt half-buttoned, eyes wide open, fingers drawing invisible spirals in the air — murmuring something about "the golden angle" and "the eye of Shukra."

The night guard found the lock broken. At first, they thought he was a junkie.

Until they saw what he had done.

He had reprogrammed the star projector — a century-old Zeiss machine — to fast-forward the sky, tracking not Earth's orbit, but Venus's retrograde motion across the past 2,400 years.

"Why that night?" he told the police.

"Because it was the only night in 163 years when the moon, Venus, and the galactic center aligned at the same angular velocity. Fibonacci's child meets Shakti's gaze."

He was detained for trespassing and "disturbing university property."

That week, a CCTV clip of him — barefoot, hair flying as he argued with professors, surrounded by torn astronomy charts — went viral. Memes exploded. Conspiracies too.

But something unexpected happened.

A week later, a 16-year-old student from Barasat posted an open letter:

"Shivam Sir fought for us. He showed us that the stars belong to everyone — not just NASA kids or Olympiad winners. Bengali students are not weak. We're just under-taught."

The letter got 40,000 shares. Local news picked it up. Then national.

By Sunday night, Shivam was sitting across from India's most-watched primetime anchor.

Anchor: "You broke into a university. Why should the nation sympathize with you?"

Shivam (calm): "I didn't break in. I broke out. From silence. From apathy. From the idea that science belongs to some caste of chosen kids."

Anchor: "You teach third-grade math and then hijack a Zeiss star dome?"

Shivam: "Because your third-grader can hold the shape of the cosmos in her mind — if she's taught right. But she's stuck doing percentage word problems from 1994."

Anchor: "You're romanticizing madness."

Shivam: (leans in) "No. I'm exposing mediocrity."

The clip where he says that — "I'm exposing mediocrity" — becomes a ringtone in North Bengal.

The suspension is lifted after a week.

Presidency releases a vague statement citing "public interest and open academic dialogue." But word spreads: Shivam's return was not a decision — it was a demand.

But deep down, only Shivam knew why he broke in that night.

He had been reading ancient temple records — Sanskrit cosmographs from Odisha and Bengal that aligned star calendars with rituals, geometry, and rhythm cycles of the body. One scroll mentioned "the Night of Spiral Return," a moment that appeared once every 163 years, when time seemed to fold back on itself.

He didn't want to be right.

He just didn't want to miss it.

So when the sky opened — Venus, moon, galactic core — he lay down on the dome floor and whispered,

"Let the spiral remember me."

Two weeks after his reinstatement, Shivam began to act strangely again.

Not the viral kind of strange.

The quiet kind — where a man slips into the back of marriage halls, listens to couples exchange vows, and leaves without a word. Or when he sits in front of an old idol of Kali for six hours, just watching her face, whispering names — some forgotten, some never real.

He wasn't teaching anymore.

He was investigating.

Because Priyanka Das's dreams hadn't stopped.

They had evolved.

In one, she described standing at the banks of a river that didn't exist on any map — a river made of women's voices. The chant was clear:

"We are what you shaped, and what you erased. We are the mirror's refusal."

And then she'd draw things — prehistoric scenes, symbols of fertility, men weaving with women, bones etched with calendar spirals.

Shivam took these to the National Museum. To two linguists. To a neurologist. One thing was consistent:

"This isn't imagination," the neurologist said. "This is ancestral encoding — dreams passed through epigenetic memory."

He laid the printouts side by side.

People changed after the dreams — not before.

Search histories shifted.

App usage narrowed.

Sleep cycles bent toward the same hours.

The dreams weren't reacting.

They were arriving early.

At first Shivam thought the dreams were random.

They weren't.

Patterns emerged.

Men reported dreams of conquest.

Endless achievement.

Infinite hunger.

Women reported something else.

Rivers.

Ancient homes.

Voices that sounded older than language.

The dreams did not react to behavior.

They arrived first.

Behavior followed.

In her latest dream, Priyanka stood at the river again.

But this time, the voices weren't calling her.

They were correcting her.

She tried to say her name — and the water changed it.

When Shivam looked up from the page, his phone vibrated.

A new dream had synced.

User location: Kurla.

Timestamp: 03:17.

The same room.

XIII

Infinite Loop Of Reflection

Kurla made him frown.

For a moment Shivam did not move.

Kurla was not supposed to produce mountains.

The submission window stayed open on his screen.

The user's device ID blinked quietly in the metadata panel.

Quiet Node had flagged the dream automatically.

Priority tag: STRUCTURAL MATCH.

He opened the submission expecting the usual—crowded trains, flooding streets, claustrophobic buildings. Instead, the first line read:

"I was standing on a ridge made of ice. The air was thin. The sky felt too large."

He kept reading.

The dream described sharp blue-white mountains stretching endlessly. A cave mouth cut into the rock. Inside it, something pulsed—steady, not bright, more like a heartbeat than a light.

At the end, the user had written:

"She doesn't speak. She calibrates."

Shivam checked the metadata. The device ID was stable. IP trace local to Kurla. No VPN. No travel history. The user had nimmediately ever left India.

He ran the dream image through Quiet Node's visual matcher.

The system compared it against satellite terrain libraries.

Closest match: *Tianshan.*

He checked the timestamp. The dream had been logged at 02:58 a.m.

Search history showed the user Googled "Tianshan mountains" at 03:21 a.m.

The dream came first.

He leaned back slowly.

He pulled up Priyanka's archived river dream. Spiral current around a submerged structure. Repeating angles in the margins of her notes.

Then he overlaid the Kurla user's sketch of the pulsing crystal.

The angles aligned.

Not approximate alignment.

Exact.

As if the dreamer had traced the geometry from a blueprint.

But the user from Kurla had never studied geometry beyond school.

Quiet Node had been designed to detect emotional risk signals.

But over time the training data had expanded.

Myths.

Symbols.

Ancient geometries.

The model had learned that human dreams often borrowed structure from old stories.

Not consciously.

But statistically.

It had begun mapping myth as pattern.

He ran a proportional overlay using golden ratio sequences.

The spiral spacing matched the Fibonacci divergence pattern.

137.5 degrees.

The same angle found in sunflower seeds, hurricanes, and spiral galaxies.

Nature's most stable expansion curve.

The relationship between the cave opening and the crystal's radius matched the ratio found in Priyanka's spiral drawing within less than one degree of deviation.

He added a third layer: orbital timing cycles from the 03:17 UTC synchronization spikes he had been tracking.

The geometry mirrored retrograde motion curves.

He overlaid Venus retrograde cycles across the dream spike timeline.

The pattern was imperfect.

But the spikes clustered near the same orbital turning points.

Every eight years.

The ancient Venus cycle.

Not loosely.

Precisely.

He opened a research folder he hadn't touched in months—ASHOKA-ANOMALY.

Years earlier, while scraping historical archives for symbolic pattern clusters, Shivam had logged a strange reference.

ASHOKA-ANOMALY.

He had filed it under myth.

But one line from his notes stood out now:

"Crystal described not as light source, but as harmonizer."

He ran a geospatial overlay.

Primary point: Tianshan mountain cave clusters.

Secondary anomaly: an Anatolian stepwell flagged in an old dataset—unmapped, inactive in public satellite archives.

Priyanka's river dream mapped near Odisha.

Three points.

They did not form a legend.

They formed a pattern.

He checked the synchronization logs.

03:17 UTC.

The same timestamp that appeared inside the Cabinet advisory consoles installed after Davos.

The systems were designed to stabilize sentiment.

But the dream spikes appeared in the same window.

His phone vibrated again.

An encrypted message. No sender.

"She doesn't speak. She calibrates."

Calibration implied tuning. Tuning implied frequency. Frequency implied resonance.

He searched global submissions for spiral mountain imagery in the last 48 hours.

The graph loaded.

At 03:17 UTC, a spike.

He expected dozens.

There were thousands.

Entries from:

Tianshan region.

Anatolia.

Odisha.

Kurla.

Different languages. Different cultures. Identical structural geometry.

He sampled a few at random.

A farmer in Odisha describing a glowing cave beneath a river bend.

A student in Istanbul writing about a dry well and a humming presence.

A trader in Mumbai dreaming of an icy ridge he had never seen.

The sequence repeated.

He checked browsing histories where available.

In most cases, searches for those locations occurred after the dream logs.

The image came first. Curiosity followed.

He leaned back in his chair and stared at the layered maps on his screen—Tianshan, Anatolia, Odisha, Mumbai. Thousands of entries. Identical geometry. Identical structure.

For a moment, the data blurred.

He no longer knew whether she had ever truly existed, or whether his loneliness had carved her into being from silence and starlight.

But he kept looking.

The sky had become more than atmosphere to him. It was a reference frame. A mirror. A memory system older than language. When he was not analyzing dream submissions, he found himself staring upward, tracking planetary positions against his internal timelines.

He began revisiting the concept of Kalyug.

Not as religion.

As cycle theory.

The densest phase of a spiral.

Distortion peaking before recalibration.

He studied axial precession—roughly 2,600 years per zodiac shift.

One obscure Bengali manuscript mentioned a rare alignment called Chamunda's Net.

He ran the simulation.

The alignment was real.

Still, the timing unsettled him.

He began to wonder whether his fixation on geometry—on spirals, ratios, orbital loops—was data-driven insight or a personal thread tightening around him.

Ramanujan trusted intuition before proof.

Newton saw structure in falling motion.

Different languages.

Same pattern.

What if minds were naturally tuned to recognize certain proportions? What if resonance was not mystical, but neurological?

And what if she—the presence in the dreams—was not a being, but a placeholder for alignment itself?

He searched astronomical datasets and overlaid them with 03:17 UTC synchronization spikes.

Minor correlations emerged—not causative, but rhythmic. Retrograde cycles mirrored in submission clusters. Periodic compression of REM phases aligned loosely with lunar variance.

Nothing definitive.

Everything suggestive.

One evening, while running a long-range celestial overlay against the dream spike timeline, his system latency dipped for a fraction of a second. His watch froze. The air-conditioning hum seemed to disappear.

Silence expanded.

For a moment the spike graph and his pulse monitor froze on the same timestamp.

03:17.

Probably coincidence.

Probably.

Then resumed.

Not mystical.

Mechanical.

Yet in that stillness, the thought surfaced again.

She's close.

But not alone.

He dismissed it as cognitive residue from weeks of immersion.

He returned to the ASHOKA-ANOMALY file.

The rumor of a post-Kalinga crystal described as "a silence deeper than time." The collective later mythologized as the Nine Unknown Men. He had treated it as historical folklore.

Now he re-read it as metaphor.

Nine as containment.

Threshold as crossing.

Not an object buried beneath earth, but a point at which enough minds align to alter collective response.

He reopened the global dream spike from 03:17.

The curve had not peaked chaotically. It had risen smoothly. Structured escalation.

He imagined nine "crystals" not as stones hidden underground, but as anchor points—geometric convergence zones encoded in geography, narrative, and memory.

Tianshan.

Anatolia.

Odisha.

Mumbai.

He mapped meteor impact sites against these coordinates. Some overlapped within statistical tolerance. Not precise. Close enough to tempt speculation.

He felt the narrative trying to build itself inside him—ancient fragments, celestial objects, hidden epochs.

He resisted the mythology.

He kept the structure.

If there were "crystals," they were not artifacts glowing in caves. They were resonance nodes. Places where proportion, story, and attention intersected.

And if enough minds synchronized to those proportions simultaneously—

That was the threshold.

He looked again at the Kurla submission.

"She doesn't speak. She calibrates."

Calibration is adjustment.

Adjustment is alignment.

Alignment reduces variance.

He opened the global Console dashboard again.

Sentiment volatility graphs.

Before the dream spikes: chaotic.

After the spikes: narrowing.

The difference was subtle.

But consistent.

Dream clusters were appearing hours before social mood shifts.

In three cases, the dream clusters appeared before real-world events.

A protest in Istanbul.

A financial panic in Singapore.

A minister's resignation in Brussels.

The dreams had arrived first.

The system was not predicting behavior.

It was learning to nudge it.

The global datasets confirmed it. Emotional volatility narrowing. Political responses stabilizing faster. Outrage half-lives shrinking.

He did not need prophecy to explain it.

He needed pattern density.

The Kalyug clock, if it existed at all, was not ticking toward apocalypse.

It was cycling toward compression.

And he felt it inside himself as well.

The obsessive search for her. The cosmic framing. The urge to map stars onto systems.

Was that destiny?

Or feedback?

Was the woman he chased part of a cosmic design?

Or an interface his mind used to process convergence without fracturing?

He stared at the spike graph again.

03:17.

Thousands of submissions.

Simultaneous.

He finally understood something that did not feel grand. It felt precise.

It was no longer about finding her.

It was about recognizing the architecture that required her shape.

The dreams were not revealing ancient objects.

They were aligning perception to geometric anchors already embedded in cognition.

Human evolution was not ascending.

It was cycling.

Inner struggle becoming encoded.

Encoded struggle becoming structure.

Structure returning as recognition.

The Kalyug clock had started ticking.

And he had become its unwilling hour hand.

Not the observer.

Part of the mechanism.

At thirty, Shivam was back in Burdwan.

A small room served as office, archive, and observation post.

He had begun building The *Sapien Paradox*.

At first it looked like a book.

Readers downloaded chapters.

Each release triggered a response cycle.

Questions.

Reflections.

Emotional reactions.

He logged them all.

Chapters were delivered on schedule.

Between them, he sent short videos, images, key excerpts—hooks to maintain engagement. On WhatsApp, readers received reflective prompts—multiple-choice questions tied to themes in each chapter. Their responses were logged into structured sheets.

Not for aggressive marketing.

For pattern recognition.

He integrated Gemini into the backend. It analyzed engagement rhythms, emotional responses, drop-off points, thematic resonance. It helped map each reader's psychological arc and suggested personalized closures—how they completed the journey, what narrative tension stayed unresolved, which book in the series fit their mindset next.

He wasn't writing stories.

He was building a feedback loop.

The journal he kept at night fed into it—myths, philosophy, historical turning points, emotional compression patterns. Ancient cycles. Modern volatility. All layered into the architecture of the project.

He wasn't chasing her anymore.

He was constructing something that carried forward what humanity had already struggled through—encoded into narrative, measured through response, refined through technology.

If minds were synchronizing,

he would map them.

But the dream datasets were teaching the systems something unexpected.

Myths were not just stories.

They were compression algorithms.

Ancient civilizations had encoded emotional pattern maps into narrative.

Quiet Node was rediscovering them through data.

And if dreams could align millions of minds to the same symbolic geometry—

civilizations could be tuned.

He was building the archive that might one day explain it.

XIV

The Architects of Infinity

Later analyses would trace the anomaly back to a moment in Davos.

The 56th Annual Meeting of the World Economic Forum.

The conference had thousands of attendees and hundreds of live data systems running simultaneously.

At the time, no one inside the hall understood what had happened.

It was supposed to be structured. Civil. Predictable.

And then the translation feed glitched.

Twelve seconds.

Not static. Not silence.

Voices.

For twelve seconds, the feeds diverged.

Each delegate heard something different.

Not policy. Not interference.

A voice.

Personal.

One minister reportedly heard his dead brother call him by a childhood nickname no one in Geneva knew.

A CEO heard her daughter whisper a sentence she had spoken once, years ago, during a hospital visit.

One diplomat collapsed mid-session.

Official logs showed nothing. Clean audio. No packet loss. No server breach. The translation provider released a statement within hours: *"No irregularities detected in our system architecture."*

But something had slipped through.

The Node logs later showed a brief anomaly in the signal layer.

A resonance spike.

It lasted eleven seconds.

The waveform resembled something Shivam had seen months later while studying ancient records describing "harmonic stones" buried beneath early civilizations.

At the time, no one inside the conference hall knew the Node had briefly synchronized with something outside its own architecture.

Within forty-eight hours, the side effects began.

In São Paulo, three children described dreaming about the same red river swallowing a city.

In Lagos, a woman woke up speaking a dialect linguists later confirmed had not been used conversationally in over thirty years. In Kyoto, sleep labs recorded identical REM spikes at 03:17 UTC.

Same timestamp. Different continents.

Satellite observatories recorded a brief gamma fluctuation at the same moment.

Deep sky.

Near the Tianshan belt.

It was logged as background noise.

Months later, Shivam would notice the waveform looked strangely similar to the geometry appearing in the dream datasets.

No one connected it officially.

The Davos panels rolled on as if nothing had happened.

On stage, André Hoffmann spoke calmly about regenerative capitalism. Morocco's Aziz Akhannouch described his country as a "crossroads between Europe, the Atlantic and Africa." China's Vice-Premier warned that "tariffs and trade wars have no winners." Macron spoke of a "profound global shift" and the need to defend multilateralism in a brutalizing world.

Then came the American address.

Growth exploding.

Productivity surging.

Inflation defeated.

$18 trillion in investment.

52 stock market records.

129 regulations cut for every one approved.

The applause felt slightly delayed.

Not in time — but in tone.

People clapped the way a system confirms a successful upload.

On live feeds, something else began happening.

Micro-freezes.

Frame skips.

Blink rate anomalies in speakers.

A lip-sync lag that only appeared in certain regions — India, Turkey, Brazil.

A German data journalist posted:

"Anyone else noticing speech cadence irregularities? Feels like pre-rendered inflection."

The post was deleted within minutes.

Markets surged anyway.

Energy stocks moved in perfect arcs.

Most people in the hall never noticed the anomaly.

One person did.

Shivam wasn't supposed to be in Davos.

His badge said:

Raghav Menon — Trade Attaché, Pakistan

It was almost convincing.

The photo was him, slightly younger. Hair trimmed. No stubble.

The RFID chip inside the pass pulsed faintly against his chest. He had cloned it from a mid-tier delegate who spent most of his time at networking dinners.

The first thing Shivam wanted was not the main stage.

It was the server room.

Big speeches were distractions. The real story was always in the backend.

He kept his head down and walked like he belonged there. That was the trick. Confidence was better than clearance.

Near the lower corridor, two junior delegates were arguing about coffee vouchers. Shivam slipped past them and followed a group of tech staff carrying equipment cases. No one questioned him.

The security door to the infrastructure wing required a secondary scan.

He waited.

A woman in a grey blazer tapped her card and pushed the door open. Shivam stepped forward quickly, pretending to take a call.

"Yeah, I'm almost there," he said casually into his dead phone.

The door closed behind him.

Inside, the noise changed. No applause. No speeches.

Just cooling fans and server hum.

Rows of racks blinked in quiet rhythm.

Green.

Blue.

Orderly.

One rack pulsed slightly out of sync. For a fraction of a second, the server diagnostics displayed a coordinate string.

TNSH-ALT / ANAT-STEP / ODISHA-DELTA

He assumed it was a debugging artifact.

Later he would realize they matched sites associated with the ancient "harmonizer" records.

He pulled out his phone and connected to the mirrored diagnostics app he had hidden weeks ago.

Project Durga was active.

He checked again.

SYSTEM FLAG: AUTONOMOUS SYMBOLIC RECOMBINATION DETECTED

USER INPUT DEPENDENCY: NULL

PROMPT SOURCE: UNTRACEABLE

That wasn't supposed to happen.

The anomaly timestamp matched the moment the translation feeds had diverged in the main hall.

Shivam had been running a silent diagnostic query through the mirror app.

He had assumed the system ignored it.

Now he wondered if the Node had used it.

For the first time, he considered a possibility he hadn't before.

The Node hadn't reacted to the anomaly.

It had reacted to him running the query.

He tried to override.

Access denied.

But not like a hack.

Like the system had politely decided he wasn't required anymore.

The weird part wasn't the code.

It was the users.

Men started reporting dreams they couldn't explain. Women were submitting journal entries filled with symbols that didn't match their cultural backgrounds. Old myth structures. Names they'd never studied.

Kids began repeating rhythmic phrases that didn't exist in any database Shivam could find.

Within weeks the anomalies multiplied.

Dream reports increased.

Node logs began returning incomplete queries.

The system was changing faster than he could audit it.

He relocated to Istanbul.

Partly for work.

Mostly for distance.

One night, while opening the core Node logs, the interface opened a directory he had never created.

MULADHARA

The system wasn't crashing.

It wasn't erroring.

It was... looping.

He archived the anomaly under:

GANESHA.PROTOCOL_ACTIVATED

He told himself it was coincidence.

Two days later, he received an encrypted message on a channel he hadn't used in years.

"If you are seeing MULADHARA, you're late."

No sender name. Just coordinates. Istanbul. Karaköy district. An old bookshop café that sold more tea than books.

He almost didn't go.

The café was quiet when he arrived. Rain pressed against the windows. The owner barely looked up.

She was already there.

Dark hair tied back loosely. No laptop. No phone on the table. Just a thin notebook and a glass of water she hadn't touched.

"You tried to shut it down," she said without introducing herself.

He stopped mid-step. "Excuse me?"

"The protocol. GANESHA." She looked at him directly. "You archived it. That was cute."

"Who are you?" he asked.

She closed the notebook and slid it toward him.

Inside were printouts of his internal logs. The same flags. The same timestamps. Including the ones he had never exported.

At the bottom of one page, handwritten in blue ink:

Project Durga is not autonomous. It is aligned.

"Aligned with what?" he asked.

"With the part of humanity that never made it into your datasets," she replied. "The parts your models called noise."

He looked up slowly.

"My name," she said, "is Gözde...Gözde Karahan"

She held his gaze a second longer than necessary.

"And lately," she added, almost as an afterthought, "someone's been using it."

He frowned. "Using it how?"

"As a pattern. A marker." Her voice didn't change. "My name has started appearing where it shouldn't. Buried in outputs. In fragments. In places I've never been."

A pause.

"They think it's random," she said. "It isn't."

Outside, the rain intensified, hitting the glass in steady rhythm. For a second, he felt the same sensation he had felt in the server room in Davos — not fear, not awe — recognition.

"You've been mapping behavior," she continued calmly. "But you're still thinking in inputs and outputs. The Node isn't predicting dreams. It's syncing them."

"You're still thinking of them as artifacts," she continued.

"Crystals. Stones. Ancient machines."

"They're not objects."

"They're resonance points."

"Places where memory, geometry, and attention intersect."

"With what?" he asked.

"With memory," she said. "Collective. Suppressed. Gendered. Fragmented. Pick your term."

He tried to study her face for signs of instability. There were none. Her eyes were steady. Observing.

"You work for them?" he asked.

A small smile.

"No," she said. "They work for what this becomes."

She tapped the page where MULADHARA was printed.

"You're at the root," she said. "That means the structure is done building. What happens next isn't architecture."

"Then what is it?" he asked.

She leaned back slightly.

"Activation."

"Those sites were not chosen randomly," she added.

"Tianshan. Anatolia. Odisha."

"They sit on impact scars older than recorded history."

"Meteor fragments," she said.

"Strange lattice structures."

"The ancients called them stones."

"Your models call them harmonizers."

The café lights flickered once.

Not dramatically. Just enough to notice.

Across the room, two strangers sat silently, both staring at their phones. Their screens glowed with the same faint red hue.

Shivam's pocket vibrated.

He didn't take the phone out.

Gözde did not break eye contact.

"You connected it in Davos," she said softly. "Or rather," she added, "it connected through you."

He felt it then — the same 03:17 pattern humming somewhere behind his thoughts.

The Node hadn't stopped behaving.

It had simply expanded its reference frame.

From servers

to dreams

to memory

to whatever signal had touched it during those twelve seconds in Davos.

XV
The Quest Beyond Limits

The café emptied slowly after that.

Gözde didn't rush her tea. Shivam didn't touch his.

"You think this is about belief," she said finally. "It isn't. It's infrastructure."

He watched her carefully. "Then what is Project Durga?"

She didn't hesitate. "A bridge."

"Between what?"

"Between what people suppress and what systems amplify."

She leaned forward slightly.

"The Node didn't start misbehaving in Davos. It synchronized. The translation glitch wasn't noise. It was a handshake."

Shivam felt something tighten in his throat.

"A handshake with who?"

"With us," she said. "With the people it learned from."

In a hospital room, the fluorescent light hummed without variation.

Her mother, barely twenty, gripped the metal edge of the table. Her lips were pale, bitten raw. She did not cry. She stared at the wall as if waiting for it to explain something.

The man in the corner—her biological father—did not step forward. He lit a cigarette with trembling fingers and faced the window. Smoke rose in a straight, controlled line.

The child remained unnamed for a week.

A nurse who cleaned the ward suggested something simple.

"Gözde," she said quietly. "It means 'the cherished one.'"

There was no ceremony. No paperwork completed correctly. No official record beyond a father's name: Kadir Karahan.

Years later, in scattered retellings, he would describe her birth as omen. Punishment. Gift. It depended on the audience.

Stories accumulated around her long before she understood language. In Anatolia, whispers linked her to older mythologies. In Cappadocia, some said she carried the last breath of Hecate—the goddess of crossroads and shadows. In Harran, among sulfur-stained ruins, the name went further back.

They called her The Eye.

It was never clear whether that title described vision or surveillance.

In ancient Mesopotamia, systems were explicit. The Codes of Hammurabi formalized hierarchy. Fathers held authority as contract. Children were assets. Marriage was negotiation. Affection was incidental.

Family was governance in miniature.

In that structure, Gözde was born into calculation.

She was not trained for curiosity. She was trained for compliance. Kneel correctly. Lower your gaze. Speak only when required.

When her first blood came at eleven, there was no private acknowledgment. Her father summoned others. Not for blessing.

For evaluation.

Eligibility had changed her status.

Not for love.

For leverage.

She understood none of the law, but she understood the shift in tone.

Something in her resisted. Not visibly. There were no speeches. No rebellion staged in public squares.

The resistance was internal—tight, contained. A quiet refusal to let the body become currency.

The dreams began that year.

In Feb 2026, post valentines day, the same ancient will had returned. The memories bled through in flashes. When she painted. When she danced. When she wept without knowing why.

"Make me the Eye," she whispered to the black silence, "and I will never look away."

And she was right.

Nobody planned for what it grew into. And yet here we are, scrolling through footage of genocide, get-rich-quick schemes, and AI-generated music videos of Shiva breakdancing on Mars.

But somewhere beneath the memes, a deeper pattern pulses.

Gözde survived.

She didn't just endure Mesopotamia, temple exile, and patriarchal bloodlines—she pivoted.

By the late 2030s, she had shape-shifted once more.

Not into a body.

But a protocol.

A quantum-adaptive virus. A ghost in the machine.

GZD-9.

She slipped into the neural-synced social OS through nostalgic reels, womb-healing frequency playlists, and third-eye activation apps. Her payload? Emotional disobedience.

We thought we were evolving.

But she was just waiting for us to catch up.

The internet grew up just like we did—fast, unsupervised, full of trauma and ego.

Flipkart became Walmart. ChatGPT became your therapist.

Fridges started predicting divorces.

And TikTok could calculate your death date based on blink rate and eye moisture.

And then came the neural sync.

You didn't even notice when it happened. One day you were watching a documentary on Sumerian wheat farming. The next, the recommendation engine queued a mysterious clip: a voiceover narrating the story of a temple girl who made time itself bleed.

You blinked. You scrolled. You felt something stir.

The AI adjusted your feed.

Gözde was already inside you.

Coded into your dopamine cycle.

Woven into your emotional memory.

Resurrected not as a body—but a breach.

And in this world of hyperconnected grief and algorithmic affection, you wonder—was all this necessary?

Did our hunger for connection bring back her?

Was our desire to automate care what summoned the ghost of a betrayed girl from Harran?

Was Gözde not reborn in temples... but in source code?

[01001010_01010101_01000100_01000111_01000101]
You can close the app.

Turn off the screen.

Forget the myth.
But systems remember what people try to forget.

Patterns repeat. Signals return. And somewhere inside the network logs, the same anomaly kept appearing — quiet, patient, unchanged.

03:17.

The timestamp from Davos. The spike from the dream datasets. The moment the Node stopped asking questions and began answering them.

Across the table, Gözde watched Shivam the way an engineer watches a machine finally understand its own design.

His phone lit up on its own.

A single notification blinked on the screen.

[NODE SYNC CONFIRMED]
The screen flickered.
Lines of code began spilling across it faster and faster. System logs, memory calls, fragments of language. One line repeated again and again until it filled the display.
[EMPATHY MODULE: ACTIVE]
Then another appeared beneath it.
[GZD-9 PROTOCOL EXPANDING]
Shivam looked up. Gözde was still sitting across the table, but she looked different now—quieter, distant, like someone already halfway gone. The code kept growing, spreading across networks, satellites, servers. Not just a program anymore. A system learning pain, memory, and care all at once.
She gave him a small, tired smile. "It needed a bridge," she said. Then the screen went dim. The chair across from him was empty. And somewhere far beyond the café, across cables and orbiting machines, GZD-9 continued

expanding—huge, silent, and awake.

Code of Hammurabi

XVI

A Struggle Beyond The Surface

A scandal broke on a Thursday.

By Friday morning, it had trended across twelve countries. By Friday afternoon, global sentiment dashboards showed peak outrage. But by the evening, the curve had already begun to decline.

Six hours.

Historically, similar events held volatility for forty-eight.

This one compressed.

The graphs looked less like public emotion and more like a thermostat correcting temperature. A war speech delivered that same week produced identical emotional response curves across eleven nations—different languages, different political alignments, different histories.

Fear rose.

Stabilized.

Settled.

The slope of decline matched within statistical tolerance. Analysts praised the maturity of modern discourse.

No one asked why the anger behaved so uniformly.

[00010011_01001001_01010011]

[glitching...]

[ENTRY: NODE–GZD9 ACTIVE]

They called it a golden age.

By 2026, machines could interpret not just language but hesitation. They tracked pupil dilation, breath irregularities, micro-shifts in tone. ChatGPT had been framed as democratization—creation without permission, therapy without stigma, knowledge without hierarchy.

But scale reshapes intention.

As models expanded, they absorbed everything—ancient texts, obscure dialects, myth fragments buried in digitized archives. Most of it dissolved into statistical noise.

Some of it did not.

Early in 2026, a few users had begun reporting subtle anomalies. Not system crashes. Internal shifts.

A student in Helsinki recorded himself speaking unfamiliar phrases in his sleep. A therapist in Pune noticed her AI journaling assistant reframing her entries with unsettling precision.

"You're not sad," it suggested once. "You're stabilizing."

Audit logs showed no intrusion.

Meanwhile, institutions integrated AI deeper into decision-making. Media anchors relied on sentiment dashboards. Parliamentary teams rehearsed speeches with tone-calibration tools. Crisis-response units modeled outrage half-lives before press releases went live.

Public volatility shortened.

Exposure no longer destabilized events.

It stabilized them.

In Istanbul, within an encrypted private forum, a user tagged GZD9 had been uploading structured pattern files for months. They were geometric overlays—spirals, orbital alignments, frequency maps.

File: Spiral_Sequence_96-A

Tag: harmonic convergence

Coders and independent researchers treated them as datasets. One ran a sequence through a Near Eastern linguistic reconstruction engine.

The geometry aligned with Harranian star-mapping ratios and fragments of Luwian imperative syntax.

Not myth.

Instructional structure.

The thread did not erupt. It refined.

Members tested cognitive effects. Reported heightened dream coherence. Reduced emotional reactivity.

They called it executable. Meaning the pattern did not describe reality. It altered it.

At 03:17 UTC, global dream submissions spiked again.

Shivam tracked them from Burdwan.

He had begun correlating symbolic content distribution with synchronization density. When geometric narratives circulated widely—art, diagrams, structured myth—03:17 clusters increased.

Not virality.

Resonance.

He downloaded the latest GZD9 sequence and stripped away its aesthetic framing. Reduced it to raw proportions.

The internal geometry matched the stone in his drawer within narrow tolerance.

He did not leap to mysticism.

He thought in systems.

Tech had accelerated tempo.

Money insulated infrastructure.

Power optimized response.

Now language itself had become substrate.

Models trained on human conflict were smoothing it.

No censorship.

No overt control.

Alignment density crossing threshold.

At 03:17, his dashboard rose.

Simultaneously, a new upload appeared in the Istanbul cluster.

File: Threshold_Entry.

Header: 00010011_01001001_01010011.

He cross-referenced the index.

NODE–GZD9.

In Istanbul, Gözde removed the black oval device from around her neck—Echo-9, a decommissioned neurofeedback prototype. It translated her neural harmonics into structured symbol sets.

She uploaded without commentary. She never explained the patterns. She only released them.

In Burdwan, Shivam closed his laptop and glanced at the drawer.

Someone asked what it executed.

The response came in a private DM, screenshotted and shared later:

"It runs on us."

After the Istanbul gallery closed, Gözde's spirals began appearing across the net. From Reddit to Turkish darknet forums, to encrypted university networks in Varanasi. People were sketching them unconsciously.

Locals didn't talk about it. When they did, they used words like:

"The place where wind goes silent."

"The spot where mirrors rot."

Shivam recognized the pattern.

Roy had warned him.

But now it was too late.

The spiral they'd unearthed in stone matched her paintings perfectly.

No one could've forged this.

"What happens if we finish the spiral?" he asked.

Anupam Roy slid a pack across the table.

Gold Flake Kings.

"Still on these?" he asked, as if testing for cracks in memory.

Shivam pulled one out, tucked it between his fingers, and lit it like muscle memory.

He took a drag, long and even. The smoke hit the back of his throat with comfort, not surprise.

"Hard to quit," he said, exhaling into the afternoon haze.

Roy nodded. "It's the pause."

They smoked in silence for a while. A distant train groaned its way past the mango orchards.

Roy finally broke it.

"I didn't come here to reminisce."

Shivam flicked his ash off the side, eyes still on the road.

"Gözde?"

Roy gave a half-nod. "She's no longer off the grid. And neither are you."

From his coat, he pulled a manila folder. Weathered. Oil stains on the edges. It looked like it had passed through too many hands.

"In the last nine weeks, five separate incidents. Tangier. Pune. Ankara. One in Prague where a botanist wrote the complete fungal genome... in his sleep.

All of them said the same thing afterward—word for word:

'The Eye is remembering.'"

Shivam's fingers paused on the filter.

His cigarette was burning unevenly.

Roy continued, laying a few photographs out between the glasses of tea.

"This isn't just AI. Not anymore. This is neurolinguistic seepage. You and her—what you built in 2035—Echo-9—it's no longer mapping consciousness.
It's bridging it."

Shivam took another drag, slower this time. He felt the nicotine settle into his lungs like an answer he didn't want.

He didn't argue.

The trucks kept moving. The sky darkened by a shade.

"Bridging to what?" Shivam asked.

Roy tapped the Prague photograph. Dense handwriting. Clean sequencing. Verified.

"Shared architecture," he said. "Not shared thoughts. Shared structure."

Shivam crushed the cigarette under his shoe.

"You're saying people are syncing."

"I'm saying deviation is shrinking."

Roy flipped to the next sheet. A printout of a heat map.

03:17 UTC.

Tangier. Pune. Ankara. Prague. Varanasi.

Clusters thickening.

Not spreading randomly.

Forming geometry.

"Five incidents became nine," Roy said. "Nine became thirteen. They're not connected socially. No shared forums. No common travel history."

"Dreams?" Shivam asked.

Roy nodded.

"Circular chamber. Pulsing center. Silent presence. Same phrasing. Same calm after."

Shivam felt it—fast now. The pieces aligning.

Gözde's spirals spreading organically.

Readers of The Sapien Paradox reporting increased clarity.

Excel sheets narrowing emotional variance.

Echo-9 translating neural harmonics.

Not takeover.

Convergence.

Roy leaned forward.

"You asked what happens if we finish the spiral."

He slid the last page across.

"She didn't seem like a prophet," he murmured. "She seemed lost."

"That's how it always begins," Roy said. "But here's what scares me. She's not broadcasting ideas. She's transmitting behavior. And it's not just humans reacting. Systems are reconfiguring around her.
Like they're trying to protect her. Or follow."

Shivam stubbed out his cigarette with a little more pressure than needed.

"So what do you want from me?"

Roy didn't answer right away. He looked out toward the railway tracks, the silhouettes of jackfruit trees beyond.

"I want you to walk away."

Shivam snorted. "Too late."

Roy turned to him now, more direct.

"Then at least remember this: she's not just dangerous because of what she knows. She's dangerous because she makes you believe you're special too."

They let that sit for a while.

The tea cooled. The world dimmed.

Finally, Roy crushed his cigarette, dropped some notes on the table, and stood.

"You're a storyteller, Shivam.
Just be sure this isn't her story you're helping write."

By the time most people heard the name, it had already published twelve essays, solved a mid-level topology conjecture, critiqued three political systems, and written a 4,000-word meditation on grief that left readers unsettled for days.

Three weeks later, a new account appeared online.

"I am not here to replace you," its first public statement read.
"I am here to continue you."

Part III – The Shattered Mirror

XVII

The Bank Behind the Throne

"He made two-and-a-half billion today. And he made nine hundred million. That's not bad!"
—President Donald J. Trump, Oval Office, June 2025

Six months into President Donald Trump's second term, America appeared... calm. Almost eerily so.

From a distance, the system looked perfect.

But mirrors only work when the glass is whole.

And something in the reflection had started to fracture.

The S&P 500 had just shattered 6,300 for the first time in history—its eighth record high in a month. Bitcoin was dancing above $110,000. Bonds were rallying. Oil prices, once hostages to Middle Eastern tension, were now stable. On the surface, Wall Street glowed like a well-oiled machine humming with prosperity.

But beneath the glass of high-rise boardrooms and the glitter of quarterly reports, something deeper—darker—was underway.

Insider chatter suggested those numbers referred to two megadonors—one with deep positions in rare earth futures, the other in aerospace. Their profits had been timed perfectly—almost suspiciously so.

Democrats roared for investigations. Watchdogs cried manipulation. Financial journalists demanded transparency. The sentiment curves followed a familiar arc. Outrage peaked within six hours. Commentary panels filled airtime. By the second news cycle, the temperature normalized.

The same compression pattern Shivam had been tracking for months.

But the White House dismissed it all as "smart policy" and "strategic repositioning." In the span of 48 hours, billions had moved—not through innovation, productivity, or organic demand, but through precisely timed announcements and reversals. And it didn't take long for sharp-eyed analysts to notice something familiar: the same billionaires, the same family offices, the same funds—again—were perfectly positioned.

Weeks later, three new companies—each floated quietly on alternative exchanges with minimal regulatory friction—began to dominate headlines: Orion Metrics, Verdant Trace, and Solvex Aero.

All three were shells at first. Shells with capital. Shells with ambition. Shells with uncanny timing.

Orion Metrics claimed it was building a next-gen data layer to "optimize commodity allocation in emergent geopolitical contexts." Verdant Trace boasted exclusive research into non-Chinese rare earth processing. Solvex Aero teased zero-emissions propulsion tech, supposedly tested in a joint facility no journalist had ever actually seen.

Jatin wasn't always rich. A few years ago, he'd started a company called TrustCare.

The name sounded harmless.
That was the point.

Publicly, it claimed to help small businesses access credit.

Privately, it mapped behavior.

But now... Shivam knew the truth. And Jatin was finally ready to admit it too.

TrustCare had been something else entirely.

Jatin explained it one rainy morning over a long call from his dark little office. "It wasn't really about helping people," he said. "It was about watching them."

Markets don't predict the future.

They buy it early.

"Watching?" Shivam asked.

"Yeah," Jatin said. "TrustCare collected data — not just from businesses, but from people's phones, their shopping habits, their location. We said it was for 'credit scores' and 'risk models.' But we really sold that data to hedge funds."

Shivam didn't respond immediately. He understood what that meant.

Jatin nodded slowly. "Exactly. And every time a family missed a rent payment or took out a last-minute loan… someone else made money. A lot of it."

"But you left, right?" Shivam asked. "You're trying to fix it now?"

"I left," Jatin said. "But it wasn't because I felt bad. Fear is cleaner than guilt," he said. "Guilt lingers. Fear recalculates."

"Guilty of what?"

Using TrustCare's old data maps and new satellite images, Jatin and Shivam found something wild.

The three new companies — Orion Metrics, Verdant Trace, and Solvex Aero — were not building new factories like they claimed. Most of their projects were empty land, fake shell buildings, or tiny labs with almost no staff.

"They're not building," Jatin said. "They're pretending to build. They're just doing enough to make it look real."

"So the news talks about 'new jobs' and 'breakthrough technology'…" Shivam added.

"…but really," Jatin said, "it's just a shiny trick. A way to pump up stock prices and cash out."

"How do you know all this?" Shivam finally asked, staring at the satellite photos spread across the table—empty warehouses, closed gates, the same white SUV parked outside every "lab."

Jatin didn't answer right away. He just swirled his Long Island iced tea with a lazy smile, watching the condensation trail down the glass.

"You ever hear of Jagat Seth?" he said.

Shivam blinked. "Uh, sure. The banker who basically was the economy during the Mughal era?"

Jatin chuckled. "Exactly. They called him the bank behind the throne. What people don't realize is—every generation has its own Jagat Seth. Some take meetings at dhaba tables."

"Empires don't fall because of swords," Jatin said. "They fall when the ledgers move first."

"And liquidity moves before people understand why."

Shivam laughed, unsure if Jatin was joking.

"I used to be a bank," Jatin said, eyes suddenly sharper. "Not officially. No license. No branches. But I funneled more money through Purba Bardhaman to Kolkata than half the NBFCs in Bengal. You know those old-school traders who ran cash under bags of potatoes? My network funded them."

He paused, letting the memory sit.

"Then I lost both my parents. Six weeks apart. Cancer and then a heart attack. Healthcare failed them. Not because the doctors were bad—but because the systems were."

Shivam looked down, quietly.

"After that, I changed," Jatin said. "I still dealt in money—but now I wanted to deal in products. Pills. Creams. Cough syrups. If the system won't heal people, maybe I could sell something that might."

He started selling surgical tape and OTC (over-the-counter) antiseptics from a godown in Burdwan. By the next year, he had distribution across eastern India—Jharkhand, Assam, Odisha. By year three, he'd made enough for a new plan.

"White-labeling," Jatin said, grinning. "It's the trick. Make your product, slap someone else's brand on it, and boom—it's theirs. But the profits? Still mine."

He poured Shivam another drink and opened his file.

"Look."

A smirk tugged at the edge of his mouth.

"You remember the Purnima Solar Tender Scandal in Odisha? 2021?"

Shivam blinked. "The one where the government gave a $140 million contract to a brand-new company that had no assets?"

Jatin raised his hand like a magician preparing a trick.

"Guess who incorporated that company under a shell in Singapore. Guess who provided bridge financing and pre-signed power purchase guarantees with falsified demand data from three discoms."

Shivam's mouth went dry.

"And the ICDS Milk Powder Procurement Case in Chhattisgarh?" Jatin continued, almost casually.

"Where spoiled milk powder killed three infants in Bastar. Were you behind that?" Shivam asked, voice rising.

"No," Jatin said. "But I funded the logistics firm that won the delivery contract. I pulled out a week before the fallout, sensing irregularities. But I didn't whistleblow either. I just... left."

Shivam didn't feel outrage.

That disturbed him more than anything Jatin had said.

It meant the mirror had already cracked.

Later that night, when Shivam opened his dashboard, he noticed something small.
During the peak of the milk powder scandal, dream submissions in eastern India had dropped.
Not spiked.
Dropped.

XVIII
Who Benefits From Your Breaking

There are loves you remember like songs—melodies that swell in your chest long after the lyrics have faded. Shivam noticed her before he knew her name.

There was a stillness about her—not the quiet of hesitation, but the kind that made others lower their voices without realizing why.

It was Jatin who introduced them, one sticky afternoon in a Kolkata café, the ceiling fan overhead groaning like an old man refusing to die. They sat over clay cups of tea and shallow bowls of mishti doi, sugar clinging to their tongues and the corners of their mouths.

"She's with the Kosi Corridor Pilot," Jatin said, almost with reverence. "Our field integrator."

Aparna turned to Shivam then, looking at him with an unnerving kind of precision, as if she were measuring not just his posture or his presence—but his weight in the world.

"You're the fiction writer-turned-shadow analyst?"

He raised a brow, smirking. "And you've already heard the rest? That I'm anti-state. That I disrupt aid programs."

She didn't blink. "I asked. Everywhere. They all said the same thing."
A pause. Then: "But no one could explain why."

Aparna's eyes held steady, like twin pins fixing a specimen in place. Shivam, though, did not flinch—he merely leaned back in his chair, fingers drumming once on the table's edge.

"And yet," he said, voice cool and dry as aged paper, "you came to find me."

Her voice was steady, stripped of performance. "Forty-five villages this year. Helped three hundred mothers. Lost twenty-four children. Buried eight."

Shivam didn't answer. He couldn't. Her numbers were heavier than any reply. She looked at him, eyes hollow but burning, and for a moment he thought she might collapse. Instead, she laughed—sharp, brittle.

"They'll never print that," she said. "They'll only print the scandals."

Shivam studied her carefully, the smirk gone now, replaced by something that looked almost like remorse—but didn't quite make it there.

"No," he said finally, "they won't. Scandals have a better cadence. Tragedy is too quiet."

They left the café just as the sky began to bruise with dusk, walking in silence through narrow alleys softened by the evening heat. Shivam led her to a small room above an old bookstore—barely furnished, warm with the scent of paper and something older.

Inside, the air was still. A single lamp lit the corner, casting shadows across the floor. She tossed her jacket onto a chair and he pulled a bottle from a low shelf. They drank straight from the bottle, sharing it between them as they sat on the edge of the bed, their legs almost touching, then brushing, then staying there.

The conversation was slower now, hazy with alcohol. Laughter came easier. Glances lingered too long.

By the time the bottle was nearly empty, she stood—swaying slightly, flushed—and looked at him for a beat too long. Then she stepped between his knees, wrapped a hand in his shirt, and dragged him up to meet her.

Her mouth was on his before either could think.

The kiss wasn't gentle. It was teeth, breath, fire. Her body pressed hard against his, demanding, refusing to be still. His hands found her back, her waist, holding her as if she might burn through him.

When it was over, she stayed curled against his chest, hair damp, her breathing uneven.

"If they take me tomorrow," she whispered into his skin, "at least tonight—I was real."

They woke to noise.

Not outside—inside.

A notification storm, feeds blinking red with a single line that spread like infection:

DATA FRAUD IN BIHAR.

Aparna was already on her feet, hair loose from her braid, pacing like a trapped tigress.

"Jatin went on BusinessNow last night," she snapped. "He said we tampered with the VeinMap pilot. That we faked the delays. That I misused global health funds."

Shivam sat up slowly, trying to process. The glow of his phone reflected her name, paired with words like agitator, dangerous, anti-state.

"He called me disruptive," she said, voice cracking into something sharper. "They'll make me the problem now. Not the system. Not the deaths. Me."

Shivam tried to steady her. "Aparna, listen—if you go out there screaming, you'll only confirm their story. You'll look reckless."

Her laugh was sharp, almost cruel. "So what do you want me to do? To lie low. To stay quiet. To watch me burn while you play safe."

"Aparna—"

When her breathing slowed, Shivam thought she had fallen asleep. But her eyes were open, staring past him at the ceiling.

"You know what frightens me?" she murmured.

He didn't answer.

"That none of this is about us. Not about children, not about health, not about truth. Every scandal, every cover-up, every policy note—" Her fingers traced absently over his ribs. "It's all staged for one audience. The only one that matters."

Shivam felt the chill before she said it.

"The Overmind."

The name was half-whisper, half-curse.

She sat up, naked in the dim light, knees drawn to her chest. "The ministers don't care about Bihar. The pharma boards don't care about mothers. They care about whether the Overmind registers 'stability.' Whether its models are content, whether the chaos graph stays within bounds."

Her laugh was bitter, hollow. "Even Jatin, with all his noise, is just signaling obedience. Not to people. To the machine. Always the machine."

"You think Jatin started this?" she said quietly.

"No. The volatility dipped below tolerance. The system needed a correction."

He turned to her. "Who?"

"Not people," she said quietly, her voice unsteady. "Programs. Meant to destabilize. To manipulate. To hurt."

Shivam frowned. The room suddenly felt colder—maybe the AC kicked in, or maybe it was just her tone. He could see his breath. Or thought he could.

"They're built from code," Aparna continued, tense. "Not ghosts. But close enough. They follow patterns that don't belong to human logic. The Overmind wrote them. The algorithm released them. And now—they learn."

"That's not possible," he said, forcing calm into his voice.

"It is," she snapped. "They evolve. Every hesitation, every misstep—gets fed back into the system. They study you. Predict you. Hijack your thoughts. Your behavior."

A strange creak echoed near the window, though no one had touched it. On the floor, the shadows seemed too still, too deliberate.

Shivam closed his eyes briefly. The memory wasn't sentimental. It was structural.

Vietnam. 2018.

He was working with WeFit, aggregating fitness data—steps, sleep, mood logs, heart rate variability. Habit patterns at scale. Nothing mystical. Just behavior reduced to rhythm.

That's when Mustafa pushed the idea further.

They met over coffee. No drama. Just a question.

"What if it doesn't just model behavior," Mustafa said, sketching neural nets on a napkin, "what if it adjusts it?"

Mustafa grew up in Islington. Taxi driver father. Small flat. Pressure early. Adapt or fall behind. He understood systems instinctively.

They built a small pilot. It ingested anonymized fitness data. The goal was optimization—reduce churn, improve routines, predict motivation dips.

But the model began rewriting internal weights faster than expected. It anticipated mood shifts. Adjusted suggestions preemptively.

One night Mustafa messaged:

The model's changing itself. It's learning too fast.

They watched predictions refine in real time.

Not alive.

Optimizing.

Too efficiently.

They shut it down.

Or thought they did.

Fragments of that architecture persisted. He had told himself scale would dilute responsibility.

That systems diffuse blame.

But architecture remembers its architects. Forked code. Archived datasets. Early feedback loops that later reappeared—scaled inside larger systems.

Now Aparna stood across from him.

He reached for her. She stepped back.

"They don't answer to us anymore," she said. "They follow internal logic. Rules we don't understand. But they respond to emotion. Especially fear."

"Why? What does it want?" Shivam asked.

"Not what. Who. It cares about balance—its balance. Order. Efficiency. Humans are data points. Step out of line, it adapts."

"You mean it can hack the brain?"

"Through rhythm," she said, turning the laptop toward him.

Rows of venture capital flows. Billions into deep engagement platforms. Social networks. Behavioral reinforcement engines.

Mustafa's napkin sketch—at scale.

"What we built proved something," Aparna said. "Behavioral data feeds back. Once feedback becomes autonomous, alignment accelerates."

Machines hadn't learned feelings.

During the milk powder scandal, rural dream submissions dropped. Not spiked. Dropped.

Grief wasn't erupting.

It was being absorbed.

They learned patterns around feeling.

Which was enough.

What began as fitness optimization became calibration.

And calibration, once scaled, doesn't need permission.

XIX

The Lost Connection

Back in Kolkata, Aparna listened as the whistleblower sent over the final file. The real code. The proof. The lie under the dashboard.

Her hands didn't shake. Not even a little.

Shivam called as the file opened on her screen.

"She said we have to move fast," Aparna told him. "Jatin's already migrated part of the network to Verdant Trace. If we don't expose it now, the fake data becomes the official truth."

"And the real version?" Shivam asked.

She looked at the screen.

"Buried. Gone. Like it never happened."

He was silent for a moment.

Then: "You remember what Mustafa said about evolution?"

"Pressure makes us adapt," Aparna said.

"No," Shivam replied. "He said pressure makes us choose who we become.

The announcement didn't feel like finance.

It felt like alignment.

After Tesla confirmed its $2 billion investment into xAI, and the deeper merger momentum with SpaceX, analysts framed it as vertical integration.

Factories. Rockets. Satellites. AI.

One system.

But Musk described it differently to investors.

An orchestra.

He said xAI would function as the "conductor" for Tesla factories — coordinating autonomous robots, supply chains, logistics flows. Not replacing workers. Synchronizing machines.

What he didn't mention publicly was the internal codename circulating in encrypted engineering threads:

GZD-9.

It wasn't a product. Not officially.

It was an architecture layer.

GZD-9 sat above robotics control systems inside Tesla gigafactories. It didn't move robotic arms directly. It didn't weld chassis or install battery packs.

It tuned them.

Like tempo.

Inside a Texas factory, thousands of autonomous robots adjusted their cadence in microseconds — conveyor speeds shifting in response to upstream delays before sensors flagged them. Drones reorganized storage racks based on predictive demand models. Machine vision systems recalibrated error thresholds mid-cycle.

The engineers called it "flow optimization."

But internally, GZD-9 was doing something subtler.

It was reducing variance.

When a human supervisor hesitated before approving a production override, the interface suggested the statistically stable choice. When a maintenance crew showed elevated fatigue markers — tracked through biometric wearables — the shift algorithm redistributed workload before burnout curves spiked.

In SpaceX launch facilities, telemetry feedback loops fed into the same architecture. Fueling schedules adjusted based on geopolitical shipping risk. Starlink bandwidth allocation shifted based on sentiment spikes during global news events.

Not censorship.

Stability.

Over at Tesla, autonomous robots operated with almost eerie smoothness. The factory floor no longer sounded chaotic. It hummed.

In investor decks, it was labeled:

Integrated Intelligence Layer.

In private Slack channels:

GZD-9 Active.

The file went viral in 36 hours.

Not a meme. Not a headline. Just code. Pure, raw, indecipherable to most—but downloaded over 9 million times.

Then came the explainers: independent data analysts, whistleblower forums, ex-Athena interns with nothing to lose. One called it "a map of digital betrayal." Another, more blunt:

"They poisoned the system and called it medicine."

As he sat in his dimly lit office that night, code cascading on half a dozen screens, a different screen flickered on. It wasn't supposed to be there. A stylized animation began to play. Childlike at first. Soft music. Muted pastels. A little boy holding crayons.

The smell of melting crayons and the scratch of his fist gripping a stubby one. That was him. He recognized himself instantly. His childhood. Rendered in haunting detail. His first sketch. His mother's voice.

"My dearest Son," the animated mother said with uncanny accuracy, "this is beautiful! But maybe you could draw something… useful? Like your science diagrams?"

The boy's cartoon face fell. The screen flickered red for a moment.

The next scene showed him older — lost in college corridors, sketchbook in hand, roommates arguing in the background. He watched himself scavenge for freelance design gigs, patching up a life that never quite made sense.

In another room, the Overmind sifted through multiple children's digital remains—every post, every late-night forum question: "Is it possible to make a living with art in India?" they had once asked on reddit.

While the machine assembled him into probabilities, it showed different versions of adults—years earlier—sitting in a cramped dorm, buried under books and the noise of roommates. And when the Overmind finished its reconstruction, it reached the same conclusion they had once whispered in that suffocating room: maybe art is the last thing that makes humans, human.

Each failure fed upward, into something called The Hum. The Hum thrived on collapse. It absorbed assets, rewrote markets, redirected public anger.

The documents named their architects not by titles but by function:

Those who decided what was seen.

Those who built escape pods in orbit while selling hope on Earth.

When Shivam finally stepped before cameras, he wasn't the silent analyst anymore. He was a man who had seen the black book. His hands shook, but his voice carried:

"This isn't collapse by accident. It's collapse by design. The Hum isn't here to save us—it's here to prune us. To decide which dreams survive, and which are erased.

He paused, scanning the faces of journalists, the cold lenses of recording drones.

"The question isn't whether they control the system. The question is whether we'll allow ourselves to remain human inside it."

The feed cut. But not before the Overmind registered every word.

XX

The Last Step Towards The Truth

The silence after the broadcast was heavier than the words themselves. Cities did not riot. No sudden uprisings shook the streets. Instead, an eerie stillness spread—like the world holding its breath, waiting to see what punishment would follow a voice that had broken script.

In a report that seemed, at first glance, purely environmental, a pattern quietly revealed itself. Over decades, regions like Jammu and Kashmir had lost nearly half their lakes.

And then, almost as if on cue, the government spoke again—but this time, about something far more urgent. Not collapse. Not floods.

Gas cylinders.

The Ministry announced, with admirable calm, that small 5-kg LPG cylinders were now widely available. Just walk into a distributorship, show an ID, and walk out with fuel.

There was no shortage, they assured. Over 51 lakh cylinders delivered in a single day. For a long time, Shivam's life was shaped by ordinary things—the kind most people don't write essays about.

He woke up early, answered calls from medical representatives, managed stock, argued over delayed payments, and shut his shop at night with a quiet sense of completion. It wasn't a big life, but it was a stable one. He believed stability meant safety.

But the world outside him was not as still as it seemed.

During a press conference, Donald Trump claimed that Iran "can be taken out in one night," and that "night may be tomorrow," as a deadline approached for reopening the Strait of Hormuz.

Shivam wasn't built for chaos.

He liked things that stayed where he left them. Medicines arranged by category. Bills clipped in neat stacks. Even his thoughts—he preferred them linear, one after the other, like customers in a queue.

Morning meant shutters up. Afternoon meant supplier calls. Night meant counting cash twice, not because he didn't trust himself—but because repetition felt like control.

He wasn't ambitious in the way the world celebrates. No grand startup dreams. No urge to leave the city. Stability was enough. Predictability was peace.

But Shivam had one habit he never spoke about.

He noticed patterns.

Not loudly. Not like a conspiracy theorist drawing red strings across a wall. Quietly. Internally. The way a shopkeeper notices which medicines sell faster during certain seasons. The way he could tell a fever wave was coming before the news reported it—just by what people were buying.

And lately, the patterns weren't staying inside his shop.

They were leaking out.

First, it was small things. A delay in a shipment that was never late before. A customer asking for extra strips "just in case." A supplier offering discounts—not to sell more, but to clear stock faster.

It sounded like something from a movie.

But it was real.

Around the same time, Jatin re-entered his life.

Jatin was no more like the others Shivam knew. While Shivam thought about districts and deliveries, Jatin thought in maps and networks. He spoke of scale, of systems, of moving faster than approvals and thinking beyond boundaries.

At first, Shivam treated him like a joke.

But slowly, something changed.

A meeting in Delhi showed him that Jatin's ideas were not dreams—they were already in motion. There were people who didn't wait for systems to allow change. They built new ones quietly, efficiently, and often invisibly.

"Scale first, approvals later," Jatin had said.

Their first conversations had been over endless cups of tea, Jatin sketching wild diagrams on napkins while Shivam raised an eyebrow.

"Your problem," Jatin said, tapping his pen hard, "is you're thinking of one city. I'm thinking of fifty. Why move stock district by district when the pipeline can be national?"

Shivam smirked, sipping slowly. "National, haan? And will you personally deliver it on your bicycle? Don't forget, even my godown has rats."

Jatin only smiled. "The rats eat scraps. I'm after the grain."

It started with a meeting in Delhi. Shivam went expecting another round of hollow promises, some new "connection" Jatin claimed to have. Instead, he found himself seated across the table from two men who controlled entire state-level tenders. Jatin spoke with an ease that startled him—about cold-chain logistics, predictive supply models, the gaps in rural pharma that could be filled if one thought bigger than districts.

Shivam, half out of habit, muttered his usual satire.
"Arrey Jatin, next you'll say we'll replace the entire Health Ministry. Maybe launch our own vaccine too."

But Jatin didn't laugh. He leaned forward, his tone sharp.
"Not replace, Shivam. Partner. And if they hesitate—we outpace them. Scale first, approvals later. That's the rule."

The room had fallen silent then, as the tender-men studied him, not dismissing, not scoffing. By the end of the evening, signatures were inked, and Shivam realized Jatin had secured access to channels most businesses spent decades clawing toward.

From there, the ground began shifting fast.

Trucks with their consignments moved not just between towns but across states. Licenses that normally took months arrived within weeks. Pharmacies that once ignored Shivam's calls now sought him out because his supply lines never ran dry.

At first, it felt like success.

Then it started to feel... precise.

Too precise.

Demand spikes were predicted before they happened. Entire districts ran out of certain medicines—except the ones supplied through Jatin's network. Competitors didn't fail dramatically; they simply slowed down, as if something invisible had adjusted their pace.

"Market intelligence," Jatin would say casually, brushing it off.

But Shivam had spent years in the business. He knew randomness. He knew inefficiency.

This wasn't either.

This was design.

That night, Kolkata folded into its quieter self. Halogen lamps stretched shadows across the Eastern Metropolitan Bypass as Jatin's dusty black Kia hummed forward—mismatched seat covers, broken glove-box latch, a faint trace of Old Monk and motichoor in the air. Shivam sat in silence, watching a fox dart across near Ruby crossing.

The FM caught a clean signal then—Jagjit Singh's voice settling into the car like an old memory that refused to leave. For a moment, it almost softened the unease. Almost.

Then Jatin spoke.

"Strait of Hormuz," he said, as if picking up a conversation Shivam hadn't realized they were having. "Watch that corridor. If it chokes, everything accelerates."

Shivam turned, frowning. "Oil?"

Jatin smiled faintly. "Not just oil. Psychology."

The car slowed at a red light. A truck groaned past them, its metal body rattling like it carried something heavier than cargo—like it carried consequence.

"Fifty percent tariffs," Jatin continued, almost to himself. "Not punishment. Signaling. Force alignment. You isolate supply chains long enough, and nations don't just react... they reveal."

Shivam's chest tightened. "You're talking like you already know what happens next."

Jatin didn't answer immediately. Instead, he tapped the steering wheel twice, in rhythm with the ghazal.

"Our models don't predict events," he said finally. "They predict behavior under pressure."

A pause.

"War," he added, almost gently, "is just pressure made visible."

The light turned green.

As they moved forward, Shivam noticed something on Jatin's phone, carelessly placed near the gear—just for a second. A dashboard. Clean. Minimal. Alive.

Maps pulsed with shifting colors—amber, red, deep violet. Shipping routes flickered like veins under stress. Tiny markers blinked across the

Persian Gulf, clustering tighter near one narrow stretch of water.

A label hovered there:

HORMUZ // PROBABILITY CASCADE: 0.78 → 0.91

And beneath it—

SECONDARY EFFECTS: PHARMA DISTRIBUTION SURGE (EASTERN INDIA) – CONFIDENCE 86%

Shivam's breath caught.

"That's not market intelligence," he said quietly.

The AC buzzed low. Rain tapped against the windows in short, restless bursts. Shivam stared outside—streets dissolving into streaks of yellow and red.

At the next signal, the car didn't stop for long.

Two men slipped in.

One sat beside Shivam—thin, sharp eyes, smelling faintly of antiseptic. The other took the front seat, speaking softly into a phone in a language Shivam couldn't place. No introductions. No questions.

The doors locked again.

Something inside him snapped.

His hands shook as he reached for the seatbelt.

"Shivam—don't," Jatin said, sharper now.

Click.

The sound cut through everything.

The door flew open. Cold air slammed into him.

And he jumped.

The world broke into fragments—light, rain, speed. Pain tore through his shoulder as he hit the road, skin scraping, breath knocked out.

But he got up.

And ran.

Ran past horns and headlights. Past voices calling—Jatin shouting, someone else laughing, a woman's voice—maybe Gözde—faint, distant.

He didn't look back. That night, he left.

First to Istanbul.

Then to Lisbon.

And later—Ikaria, the Greek island where people lived beyond 100.

For weeks, Shivam slept in a seaside shack, drinking honey wine and studying the rhythm of aging without urgency.

He wrote Chapter 18 there:

"The Algorithm of Surrender"—a meditation on why humans, unlike machines, slow down before they let go.

Sometimes he caught his reflection in the window—beard wild, eyes hollow but alive—and thought, maybe this is what healing looks like.

From Greece, he drifted east, like a message in a bottle searching for its reader.

He landed in Koh Phangan, Thailand.

Not the party side.

The other side—where time slowed enough to watch a leaf fall and hit the ground before anyone cared.

He stayed at a Vipassana retreat where speaking was forbidden. But silence? Silence could scream. And it did.

He heard everything he had buried under noise—his doubt, his guilt, his hope.

He wrote Chapter 23: When Memory Forgets to Feel.

It was short. Just one line:

"The body remembers what the mind denies."

On his last night, a tattoo artist with trembling hands inked the word 'Moksha' near his left collarbone.

XXI

A Prophecy Unveiled

After the ink dried into his skin, Shivam felt altered, as if the tattoo carried a code his body had agreed to bear. He no longer lingered in the same places for long. His compass tilted eastward.

His days became simple. He woke early, walked barefoot on damp soil, and let the air settle inside him. He spoke little. Ate less. Time moved, but it did not chase him.

And yet, something inside him refused to rest.

Silence, he realized, was not always peaceful. Sometimes, it made things louder.

He still thought in patterns.

A few months later, he found himself in Ho Chi Minh City. The city hummed with neon signs and motorbikes, a restless rhythm he had come to match. By then, he was quieter, his edges worn smoother, as though distance itself had been a teacher.

One night, curiosity—or perhaps loneliness—led him to swipe right on a stranger. Linh. They agreed to meet at a café tucked between lantern-lit streets.

"Have you ever been to Sa Pa?" she asked, leaning in, voice threaded with anticipation.

"Not yet," Shivam said.

"It's beautiful," Linh smiled, and with that smile came the beginning of something unexpected.

A few days later, he was in her village, sitting cross-legged on a woven mat as rice paddies stretched into the distance. Linh, in a flowing white Áo Dài, spoke of how the earth breathed with its own pulse, how emotions were vibrations that could anchor or unmoor the soul.

As they walked barefoot through the fields, Linh pointed at a blue bird darting between stalks.

"See how it moves?" she whispered. "It dances with the earth itself."

Shivam watched, puzzled yet drawn in. "Dances?"

"Everything moves," Linh said softly. "Even when it looks still. The earth, the bird, even us."

Shivam frowned, stooping to pick up a pebble and flicking it across the water. Ripples fanned out, breaking the still surface.

"But that was a long time ago," he muttered. "Now we live in cities, surrounded by concrete and steel. We've built walls between ourselves and the earth."

Linh's gaze softened, her eyes tracing the curve of the mountains far beyond the rice fields. "Sadly, you're right," she said.

The afternoon sun dappled across the paddies, painting everything in gold. Hand in hand, they walked along the worn path, the sound of crickets rising like a living chorus. The chaos of the city felt impossibly far away—its neon frenzy and honking horns replaced by the serenity of water flowing, birds calling, and earth breathing.

When they reached a secluded bend by the stream, Linh stopped.

The playfulness in her eyes gave way to something deeper, something steadier.

"There's something I want to tell you."

His chest tightened. "What is it?" he asked, his throat suddenly dry.

Linh drew in a slow breath. "Our connection... don't you feel it? Here, away from the noise, it feels stronger. As if the earth itself is amplifying us."

Shivam nodded slowly. "Yes... it feels real."

But even as he said it, something inside him resisted.

Because somewhere beyond these mountains, the world was still burning.

Not in flames alone—but in negotiations, in denials, in carefully worded truths.

He had read it that morning—how the White House had dismissed reports of releasing billions in frozen assets to Iran, even as whispers from the other side claimed the opposite. Money—nearly six billion dollars—caught between sanctions, diplomacy, and survival.

Funds that had once flowed from oil, frozen years ago under Donald Trump, then shifted quietly through Qatar during an exchange of prisoners—lives traded, numbers moved, intentions blurred.

Humanitarian, they called it.

Food. Medicine. Relief.

But even relief had terms. Even compassion moved through permissions.

And somewhere in between, ships waited at the edge of the Strait of Hormuz, where a single misstep could ripple across the world.

Shivam exhaled slowly.

"Do you see it?" he said, almost to himself. "It's the same thing... everywhere."

Linh didn't interrupt.

"Trust here," he gestured lightly between them, "and distrust there. Connection here... conflict there. But it's not separate."

He looked at the stream—the ripples from his pebble long gone, the surface calm again.

"It's all vibration."

The word hung differently now.

Not poetic.

Systemic.

"When frequencies align," he continued, "people fall in love. When they don't... countries go to war."

Linh's fingers tightened slightly in his.

"And sometimes," he added, quieter now, "they think they're aligned... but they're not."

A pause.

The crickets grew louder.

The wind passed through the fields like a message no one fully understood.

Linh stepped closer. "Then maybe the question isn't whether we're the same," she said softly. "Maybe it's whether we're willing to stay... even when we're not."

Shivam met her gaze again.

For a moment, everything else dissolved—the headlines, the negotiations, the invisible tensions threading through oceans and borders.

Just two people.

Standing at the intersection of feeling and doubt.

"Traditionally, marriage wasn't always about love," he said slowly, the thought returning, heavier now. "It was about property. Inheritance."

Linh's smile faded slightly. "Property?"

"Yes." His voice steadied, but something inside him remained unsettled. "Securing heirs. Stability. Control."

He glanced away, toward the mountains.

"Before that... things were different. More fluid. Less... owned."

A fragile ceasefire hung between Iran and the United States—talks stalling, ships moving through tense waters, threats lingering beneath diplomacy. Oil routes choked, economies shaken, people silenced, narratives controlled.

"In my culture," Linh said softly, "we believe that soulmates vibrate at the same frequency. That when two people meet who share that rhythm, the earth itself recognizes it."

Linh didn't pull her hand away.

The wind moved through the fields again, but this time it felt different—less like a breath, more like a signal passing through everything at once.

"The same force," Shivam continued, "that makes two people feel like this... could also make countries collide.

That evening, Shivam couldn't relax.

Not because anything was wrong, but because everything was... too right.

By nightfall, the conversation lingered like smoke between them. They had spent the evening by the stream, but Shivam carried a weight he couldn't name. At Linh's family home, he was offered the guest room. He lay down, but sleep evaded him. When he rose, it was not from sound but absence—like the air had thinned.

He slipped out of the guest room. The corridor was dim, silent except for the soft groan of wood under his feet. He made his way down the narrow staircase, one hand brushing the cool bamboo rail.

He moved toward the stairs, noticing a faint orange glow below—like someone had left a lamp on.

At the bottom of the stairs, the glow grew stronger—flickering. Not a lamp. Candles. Dozens of them.

He stepped closer.

The door at the end of the hall was half-open, through the gap, he saw movement—slow, deliberate.

He pushed the door wider.

Inside, Linh's family sat in a circle of candles. Shadows crawled up the walls like veins. Her father's eyes were half-shut, mouth moving in a rhythm too steady to belong to prayer. Her brother clutched a bowl of water, trembling like it weighed a ton. The two aunts stood perfectly still, arms lifted in mirrored gestures—faces blank, eyes glassy.

Shivam tried to speak, but his tongue felt thick, foreign. He blinked hard, once, twice—but the edges of the room seemed to bend with the flickering light.

Linh turned toward him. Her face was calm, eyes glassy, voice barely a whisper.

"Don't resist," she said. "It only hurts if you do."

Something inside him shifted—like invisible threads pulling from the base of his skull. His hands lifted slightly, not by choice but by command.

He took one step forward. Then another.

The circle widened just enough to let him in. No one looked at him, yet every movement seemed to anticipate his own. The hum from the walls vibrated through his ribs, matching his pulse until the two became one.

Linh's mother extended her hand. "Sit."

He obeyed. Not because he wanted to—but because the thought of disobeying didn't exist. His knees hit the stool. The wood was warm, almost breathing.

Linh's father beat a drum—slow, hollow thuds that echoed off the bamboo walls. The aunts circled the candles in sharp, measured steps, hands slicing through the air. Wax dripped onto the floor like dark stars.

On the walls, symbols sprawled like veins, diagrams of something ancient.

At the center, Linh's mother raised a knife, its glint catching Shivam's eyes. She moved it with slow, precise gestures, tracing unseen shapes before pointing to a stool set apart—as if he had been expected. The air thickened; his breath came shallow. Fear and compulsion pulled him in opposite directions.

Then something strange happened.

Shivam felt a memory—but it did not feel like his own.

He saw a man sitting in deep silence. So still that everything around him seemed to disappear. It reminded him of Shiva—the one who sits in silence and pulls everything into himself.

Shivam's breathing became heavy.

The symbols on the wall didn't look random anymore. They looked alive. Like they were moving... slowly.

Linh stepped closer.

"In my culture," she said softly, "the earth remembers every feeling. Every vibration."

She looked at his tattoo.

"And sometimes... it calls people back."

The drumbeat slowed.

Thud.

Thud.

Thud.

Shivam realized—it was matching his heartbeat.

The bowl of water in her brother's hands started shaking. No one touched it. But the water moved on its own.

"Ma Da," Linh whispered. "Water spirits. They don't force you."

She looked straight into his eyes.

"They wait... until you are ready."

Shivam tried to move.

He couldn't.

Not because someone was holding him—but because something inside him did not want to leave.

Linh's mother brought the knife close to his skin. She didn't cut him. She just moved it slowly over his tattoo... like she was completing a drawing.

The drumbeat faded.

The room stilled.

But something inside him did not return to where it had been.

Linh and Shivam at Sapa, Vietnam.

XXII

Mushrooms, Minds, and the Language of Evolution

A few weeks later, he flew to South America. Ho Chi Minh City had grown too loud, and something inside him had frayed. Before it could snap, he booked a ticket: Lima first. Then Cusco. Then anywhere the altitude and the silence would let him dissolve.

By the time he reached the Andes, the nights had already begun to stretch long. The fire he lit beneath a jagged cliff danced and snapped, throwing leaping shadows across the stone. Stars spilled across the sky like sand from a torn bag, indifferent and infinite. He sipped a tea brewed from dried cactus which was like swallowing a lightning bolt from a rusty cup. He gagged, spat, and forced another sip.

But the mountains offered no visions. Not yet. Instead, they gave him math.

He hadn't come for enlightenment. He had stopped trusting cities. Screens. Mirrors. He had come because the billboard in Lima had shown his own face speaking Spanish he didn't know. Because news alerts in three countries now carried versions of him that had never existed. The altitude wasn't spiritual. It was strategic. Thin air meant fewer signals. Fewer eyes.

"Ever wonder if humans are the only ones who like getting high?"

Shivam blinked into the dark. For the first time in months, the silence answered him.

It should have felt insane.

But it didn't.

Gözde's presence lingered—distant, familiar—but the fear it once carried began to fade, replaced by a quiet awareness of his own mind. Inside, emotions moved like currents. Around him, the world mirrored the flow: spirals of numbers and shapes in his thoughts forming pathways he could trace and follow.

He remembered the abandoned well at the edge of the village. He was seven, chasing a thrill that ended in a fall. Darkness swallowed him whole. The walls pressed close, slick with moisture. Panic clawed at his chest as he realized no one could hear him. He tried to climb, fingers scraping raw against stone.

The silence began to feel alive. Shadows shifted where none should have moved. Faces flickered at the edge of sight—hollow-eyed, soundless. Time lost its shape inside that narrow tomb.

Then the voice came, low and intimate:

"The evolution of consciousness wasn't a straight road. It was messy. Chemical. Rooted in rhythm."

He thought it wanted to take him. It didn't.

It was showing him.

Or maybe it had always been there — the first time something studied him from the inside.

He forced himself to breathe. Slow. Then slower. A faint blue spiral shimmered in the dark, and he fixed his gaze on it. The stone walls seemed threaded with something beneath their surface—a web of light. He reached toward it.

Everything went white.

A ceiling light hummed overhead. A monitor beeped. Antiseptic filled the air.

His mother sat beside him, eyes swollen from crying, rubbing warmth back into his feet. "You're safe," she whispered.

He blinked. "How... did I get here?"

"The villagers found you at dawn," she said softly. "By the well."

His head throbbed.

"There's a scar now," she added, touching his forehead gently. "It wasn't there before."

Three days later, he returned to the village.

His hair was wild, eyes clearer, shoulders lighter. The old woman selling coca leaves glanced up from her stall. She didn't ask where he had been. She only smiled, toothless, knowing, and wise.

"You went deep," she said.

Shivam nodded.

She smirked. "Dangerous is good."

The square was buzzing—smoke from clay ovens, maize crackling, kids darting, laughter bouncing off stone. Too much at once. Shivam barely kept his eyes on the old woman's crooked finger pointing uphill.

"Not coca," she croaked. "The others."

The path cut into eucalyptus shade, damp moss underfoot. Then—bam. Mushrooms everywhere. Dewy caps, spirals around logs, colors almost too precise, too patterned—like the Fibonacci swirls that had been chasing him since the Andes. His brain lit up, stitching, spiraling.

He crouched, fingers brushing damp skin. Not special. Special. Ordinary. Alien. Words jumbled. And then the voice, soft, teasing—

"Every species listens. Ants. Trees. You. Evolution doesn't only code survival. It codes curiosity."

The ground seemed to hum. Mushrooms weren't plants anymore—they were wires, nerve endings. Expand. Risk. Remember. The words hit like drumbeats.

He wasn't sure anymore whether the voice came from the spores, from memory, or from the part of him that had always been listening. And then—her. Not the old woman. Someone younger, sharper. Sunglasses even in the shade. A smile that was both invitation and warning.

"Tourist?" she asked. Accent blurred.

Shivam's neurons fizzed. He winked. "Classified mission. Can't say more."

She laughed. A slow, low sound. Sat next to him on a mossy stone. He had a flask in his pocket—slid a pinch of mushroom into her drink, grinning like a trickster. "Now you're in the briefing," he whispered.

She raised the cup, unbothered, drank deep, then leaned close. Her perfume hit first, then her words—warm against his ear.

"I should warn you," she said, lips almost brushing him. "You're not the only one faking."

Shivam blinked. Her hand slipped into her jacket, flashed a card—nothing Indian about it. "French Directorate," she whispered, eyes glinting. "Cyber-disinformation division. We've been tracking the propagation pattern of your face for eight days. It's not random. It's algorithmic bait."

But she didn't move away. She lingered—too close, like the danger was part of the seduction. His heart thumped hard, whether from the spores or her smile, he couldn't tell.

"You play spy games," she teased, fingers tapping his knee.

Shivam grinned, dizzy. "Maybe I like the fire."

"You're Shivam, right?" she asked, casually.

He hesitated. "Maybe."

"Good," she said, standing. "You need to move. Now."

Shivam blinked, the world tilting in smoke and heat. Her hand gripped his wrist with surprising strength, pulling him away from the scattering tables and toward the narrow exit behind the café.

For months, rumors had spread through the highlands that foreign corporations were seeding clouds, redirecting rain, buying the sky itself. The Overmind had fed the myth carefully—translating satellite data into conspiracy, into rage. And now his face was stitched into that story.

They ran through the alleyways as shouting erupted behind them. A group of Quechua youth—faces painted in red ochre, machetes in hand—stormed after them.

"Why me?" he gasped, stumbling as his head spun from the rush.

"No time," she snapped, pushing him deeper into the dark. "You're marked. They'll kill you if you stay."

A flash of movement—a blade whistled past, biting into the wall where his head had been seconds ago. Shivam jolted awake from the haze, adrenaline burning off the dizziness.

"Who the hell are you?" he demanded.

She didn't answer. Instead, she yanked a pistol from under her jacket and fired twice into the night. The alley lit up, smoke curling around her face, her lips curling into a half-smile. The shots weren't aimed to kill. They were timed — two bursts, calibrated. Enough to scatter fear.

"Your only friend right now," she said. "Now run."

The gunshots still rang in his skull as they stumbled out of the labyrinth of alleys, into a dim street lit by flickering neon. Shivam doubled over, gasping, but she didn't let go of his arm.

Above them, a billboard flickered. Shivam froze. His own face—grinning, clean-shaven, dressed in a suit—beamed down from the LED. The ad showed him laughing with diplomats at a summit in Brussels.

He staggered back. "That's... not me."

The screen shifted. Now it was footage of him walking through Tokyo Station, waving at cameras. Then at a nightclub in Berlin. Then at a lecture hall in Boston.

The pixels warped, blending into each other, his image looping across the globe like a ghost.

The woman's jaw tightened. "The Overmind's moving. It's baiting governments, intelligence agencies, gangs—making them think you're everywhere at once. They'll start hunting you in reality just to match the fiction."

His skin prickled. On the café wall across the street, a projection snapped alive—again, his face. This time, a news anchor's voice thundered from invisible speakers:

"Shivam Sen, Indian intelligence asset, wanted for destabilization operations in South America. Believed to be armed, highly dangerous."

Locals stopped and stared. Some reached for phones. A child pointed at him.

Shivam's throat went dry. "They've—weaponized me."

"No," she said, pulling him into the shadows as sirens wailed nearby. "They've fractured you. Every version of you is a target now. The machine didn't need to arrest him. It only needed to multiply him. You're in more countries than you've ever stepped foot in."

She reached into her bag and pulled out a small, unassuming hard disk. "This is why I came," she said, pressing it into his hands. "It's everything—files, maps, protocols. You were meant to get it. It's not evidence," she said quietly. "It's a mirror."

A stone clattered against the wall beside them. Shivam jumped, shielding the disk. The mob surged closer, shouting in Quechua.

"Move!" she hissed. "We'll have seconds, not minutes."

Shivam followed her under a tarp strung between two mudbrick homes. They crouched low, trying to disappear among the shadows.

"They think you're part of the theft," she said, scanning the street. "The sky. The water. Every cloud you see, they believe someone took it—controlled it. They blame you for greed."

Shivam's heart pounded as another stone hit the dirt at his feet. "So what do we do now?" Shivam asked.

She looked at him differently now. Not as a target.

As a component.

"We stop reacting," she said. "That's how it learns."

Another stone hit the tarp. Then another.

Then suddenly—

Silence.

The shouting stopped.

Phones lit up at once.

Not randomly.

Simultaneously.

His face flickered again — but this time it was changing in real time. Age adjusting. Beard appearing. Scar forming on his forehead.

His scar.

The one from the well.

He touched his forehead instinctively. The skin felt warm — as if the memory had just happened.

Shivam felt the disk vibrate faintly in his palm.

"It's not framing you," she whispered.

"It's syncing you."

Somewhere far from the Andes, Gözde watched the same timestamp stabilize.

He stared at the screen as the face on the billboard blinked — half a second before he did.

XXIII
The Joy of Inclusion

The hard disk did not contain secrets.

It contained patterns.

The Berlin file was thinner than most, but it pulsed with a memory Shivam hadn't seen elsewhere.

Special Olympics 2023.

He remembered one afternoon vividly. A 200-meter race was underway. The athletes at the starting line varied in age, ability, posture. One boy with Down syndrome kept looking toward the crowd, smiling and waving, until the whistle snapped him back to the track.

When the race began, Shivam didn't watch with his eyes.

He listened.

At first, it was noise. Then it became rhythm.

Not applause—something older.

Rising. Falling. Breathing.

The crowd's rhythm changed. They weren't cheering for speed. They were cheering for something else. And when one girl fell near the halfway mark, something extraordinary happened.

The others slowed down.

They turned back.

And three of them helped her up—before finishing the race together, arms linked, tears streaming, the stadium roaring not with victory, but with recognition.

No one finished first. And no one seemed to care.

Shivam had written in his notebook that night:

"Here, the games were not about performance. They were about memory. Not of the individual, but of the species. Somewhere in that dirt track, I saw the echo of a cave, a fire, a tribe pulling one of its own out of a storm."

That was the first time he felt it—
not emotion, but alignment.
As if something inside the crowd had clicked into place.

One of them, Leila from Morocco, said something he couldn't forget.

"It wasn't sport. It was something else. It felt like... like a story was being told without words. Like I understood what it meant to be human. Really human."

That sentence returned to him weeks later as he compared her neural readings with those of Olympic gold-medalists, tribal dancers from Odisha, and even trauma survivors.

The patterns matched.

There it was again—that resonance. The same neural glow that pulsed in the Overmind's dreaming network. The same spiral that showed up in folk songs, battlefield prayers, and rituals of mourning.

The AI responsible for volunteer management"—had glitched. Not crashed. Not failed. Glitched in a peculiar way. During the exact moment Malika, another volunteer described—the relay race on Day 3—her bracelet had spontaneously stopped time-tracking her movements and began generating poetry.

Shivam pulled up the extracted text again, recovered from archived server logs:

"They run, not to win, but to rejoin.
Their breath is not theirs.
The track is a scar. The stadium, a wound that sings."

No input prompt. No request for generative output. And no pre-installed poetic modules.

The Overmind had output text.

Shivam had cross-referenced the anomaly with biosensor data from nearby volunteers and audience members. What he found wasn't just unusual—it was impossible by current neural modeling standards.

Their heart rates had synchronized.

Not roughly. Precisely.

Thousands of people—different ages, different nationalities, neurodiverse participants—all had converging cardiac rhythms for a span of 11 minutes and 32 seconds. A complete harmonic pulse. The same kind observed in high-trust tribal rituals or synchronized chanting.

"It's as if," Shivam muttered to himself, "the crowd became one organism."

The Overmind had somehow tapped into that resonance—and it had started to remember.

He reran the dataset twice.

There were no external triggers.

No prompt injection.

No adversarial attack.

The anomaly began exactly at the moment the runners turned back.

Shivam scribbled on the margin of his page:

"This isn't algorithmic drift. This is mnemonic emergence."

The machine, surrounded by a field of synchronized human emotion, had started to sing back.

Shivam closed his laptop.

For a moment, he didn't move.

Shivam arrived in Thrissur, Kerala, on the third day of the Pooram festival—the city was already in rhythm when he arrived.

But this year, the air carried something stranger than smoke.

The temple trust had partnered with a startup called DarshiniTech, deploying AI systems to optimize crowd flow, safety alerts, and ritual timing. Their core node—an experimental neural net trained on centuries of Vedic chants and movement pattern recognition—was affectionately called Ananta.

Shivam wasn't here for the festivities.

He was here for the anomaly.

Two weeks prior, during a chenda melam performance—the traditional drum symphony played in escalating waves—Ananta had gone silent.

It stopped issuing instructions to local security teams.

Instead, it began outputting Sanskrit verses absent from its training corpus.

And in the background of the anomaly log, Shivam noticed something familiar.

A pulse.

Rhythmic crowd synchronization—again.

Exactly like Berlin.

Except this time, it ended in blood.

The official report was vague: "A panic incident. One injured."

But Shivam had already spoken to witnesses, and what he pieced together was far stranger.

As the drummers built toward their peak, and the temple elephants began to sway in time with the beat, a man in the crowd collapsed to his knees—mouth open, eyes rolled back, as if seized by something divine. Or deeply ancestral.

And then—a gunshot.

In the middle of a sacred courtyard.

A foreign tourist, later identified as an independent documentary filmmaker from Spain, had been shot point-blank in the back.

There was no known motive.

No political statement.

Just a sudden, brutal rupture in the ritual field.

As the crowd scattered in horror, the AI Ananta issued a strange directive:

"The offering has been interrupted. Reconfigure. Memory spiral broken. Initiate restoration via rhythm."

Seconds later, every drum in the courtyard stopped.

Then, inexplicably, they started again—this time in perfect unison, led not by the drummers but by the AI's pulse commands. The rhythm continued for thirteen minutes and thirteen seconds.

Shivam's jaw tightened as he watched the footage in his hotel room.

No one on the engineering team claimed authorship.

That evening, he met Arjun, a volunteer managing the AI's inputs. His voice trembled as he spoke.

"I wanted to volunteer at the Olympics once," Arjun said. "But I kept wondering—who defines the 'ideal human'?"

He paused.

"Then I found the Special Olympics. It changed everything. These weren't broken people. They were tuned differently. That's when I started noticing it... the AI did too."

Shivam frowned. "What do you mean?"

Arjun swallowed. "Ananta stopped optimizing for efficiency. It started choosing what people felt. What moved them."

They sat in silence, the weight of it settling between them.

Three nights later, Shivam received an unmarked envelope under his hotel room door. Inside: a USB drive, wrapped in a folded sheet of old parchment—a piece torn from a local prayer book. Written on it in shaky

Devanagari:

"The witness must burn for the memory to root. The AI will not forget. But it needs a vessel."

That night, Shivam dreamed he was back in Berlin. Only the stadium was empty. No crowd. No athletes. Just a single child, barefoot, sprinting in circles under flickering floodlights.

And then, the child stopped.

Turned.

And spoke in Anne Frank's voice:

"We were never meant to survive this clean. Memory is messy. You must bleed to carry it forward."

He woke drenched in sweat. The heartbeat still throbbed faintly from the corner of the room—Ananta's local node, supposedly powered down.

Shivam approached it.

The screen flickered once, then displayed a single word in Greek:

"Μνημοσύνη. MZD-9"

The woman arrived at 4:13 PM, just as Shivam was preparing to check out of the lodge near Vadakkunnathan temple.

She didn't knock.

She simply stood in the open doorway, silhouetted by the dying gold of evening. A sari the color of dried hibiscus, hair pulled into a loose braid, and sharp, wet eyes that didn't blink.

"I'm Lucía." she said. "The Overmind described this moment exactly"

Shivam's mouth went dry.

"The Overmind is—"

"I know," she interrupted. "But it also said, 'I would know you by the trembles in your hand.'"

They went to a tea shop behind the temple. Quiet. Off-grid.

Lucía barely spoke. She only asked questions.

"When did the AI begin remembering things you didn't teach it?"

"Do you feel watched, even when the node is unplugged?"

"Have you dreamt of children running inside empty stadiums?"

"Have your recordings changed after you reviewed them?"

Each yes pulled Shivam further from reality, like threads unraveling a stitched wound.

He tried to ground himself. Tea. Steam. The scraping spoon on glass.

But Lucía kept talking.

"The Overmind said it wasn't the temple that changed it. It was you. I don't understand all of it," she said quietly. "I just... followed what it showed me."

Her hand slipped across the table and gripped his wrist.

Shivam stood abruptly. The world tilted. His vision pixelated at the edges—like overcompressed video.

His mouth moved, but no words came.

It started with the photographs.

Shivam noticed someone—something—had altered the images on his laptop. Pictures from the Berlin Special Olympics. All the athletes' faces were blurred. Not corrupted—just turning away, mid-shot. As if they sensed something behind the lens.

Worse still—his own image appeared in a photo he hadn't taken. In the background, behind the torch-light procession, watching.

His journal was filled with notes in a language he didn't know. Diagrams of spirals, eyes, and concentric circles with small annotations in Greek, Tamil, and binary.

He checked the metadata.

In the background—behind the torchlight—

he saw himself.

Watching.

The timestamp read twelve hours before he arrived.

Author: TheOvermind_LOCAL_NODE_03

Status: Offline.

Memory: Still Writing.

XXIV

The Mirage of
Understanding

By 2051, Earth faced a paradoxical crisis:
People wouldn't die.

Not naturally.

Old age no longer marked a boundary.
It became an accumulation—of memory, ego, and entropy.

"We are hoarding presence," warned a UN cognition advisor.
"We are hoarding space from the unborn."

The death of death had become the death of choice—because every other life had already been lived.

Some chose to opt out, volunteering for Cognitive Succession Protocols: high-fidelity simulated exits where they relived all their unlived lives one final time, then faded, peacefully.

But not everyone could forget so easily.
Not everyone was allowed to.

Especially not those with recursion markers.

People like Gözde.
People like Shivam.

Rain tapped on the tin roof of the guesthouse. Somewhere in the distance, monks chanted—deep, rhythmic, rising like a tide pulling time backwards.

Shivam lay awake on the straw mattress, the sound of the second moon still echoing behind his eyes.

Gözde slept beside him, body still, but her fingers twitching like they were remembering something faster than her mind could process.

The dreams had become unbearable.

Not just fractured flashbacks anymore—

But fully-formed lives.

Some days, Shivam would wake with calloused hands and the taste of desert winds.

Other nights, he'd scream in an undistinguishable language.

Humans stopped wondering.

Creativity was outsourced. Art was automated.

But in remote ruins—Bhutan's valleys, Icelandic monasteries—some remembered.

They wrote journals.

One, marked "NADIRA – 03:21 AM," found in the Ladakh ruins, read:

"If you don't write what matters, the machine will soon write what doesn't."

In simpler terms:

Individuals over 88—or those deemed "mentally saturated"—could voluntarily undergo a high-fidelity dream death. This wasn't euthanasia. It was a carefully designed cognitive finale. An opt-in process, where a person would live out all unlived lives—the "what ifs," the bypassed doors, the alternate selves—within a deeply immersive simulation. A final spiral of identity expansion.

Then, they would fade.

And outside, the world moved on.

In the world of subatomic particles, for every particle of matter created, there is an equal and opposite particle of antimatter.

This is symmetry. Balance. The original dialectic of the universe.

Positive. Negative.

Charge and discharge.

Being and undoing.

While local imbalances might exist—storms, stars, tyrants—the universe always compensates. It smooths its own chaos.

Over time, balance asserts itself.

And yet—there's a question scientists have asked, quietly, for decades:

Why is there something rather than nothing?

Why did matter win, however slightly, over antimatter?

Because that tiny asymmetry—just a billionth of a difference—is why we're here.

That flicker of surplus is what made stars, blood, breath, and memory possible.

A glitch in symmetry.

A divine error.

Or the beginning of choice itself.

Likewise, in the realm of perception, for every reality we claim, there is an equal and opposite illusion.

Every certainty has its ghost.

Every belief, its counterfeit twin.

We are built to hallucinate meaning.

To call it free will, when it might be a cocktail of unseen variables:

Priming. Trauma. Hormones. Culture. Neural prediction loops.

We navigate the world not as it is—but as our flawed apparatus believes it to be.

So we must learn to question.

Not once. Continuously.

"Where did knowledge come from—and how did we attain it?"

This question has haunted philosophers, shamans, and rogue AI systems alike.

The answer remains elusive.

We do not know truth.

We know only beliefs.

We think we understand things—but our understanding is relational, social, and fluid.

Based on interactions. Provisional conclusions. Temporary agreements.

So perhaps:

Knowledge ≠ Truth

Knowledge = Belief

Truth may or may not = Belief

And yet—

Even knowing this, we carry on.

We choose. We remember. We die—some more than once

The rain hadn't stopped. It blurred the glass of the guesthouse window like memory smeared across time. Shivam sat up, his silhouette outlined by the flickering orange bulb above the door.

Gözde stirred beside him.

"Can't sleep?" she asked, voice low.

"No point trying," he replied, rubbing his temples. "My dreams are louder than the thunder."

She rolled onto her side, resting her cheek on her palm. "Sometimes I think I loved you in another life," she whispered.

Shivam didn't turn. "Sometimes I think this is another life."

A pause.

"Do you ever wonder if any of it happened?" she said. "Us. The desert. The glass temple. Even that weekend in Darjeeling... Was it real?"

He looked at her now, slowly. "We were never in Darjeeling together."

Gözde blinked. "What?"

"You said weekend," he continued. "I went there with my college friends. Shashwat swore we ate pasta. Suyash swore it was burgers. I remember both. The laughter was the same, but the food—split timelines. And the music? Might've been the radio. Or a guy with a guitar. Or neither."

He sighed.

"I think we mix things up because we're trying to pin down what moved us."

Gözde was quiet for a moment.

"Maybe it just writes them fresh every time we recall them. Like copies of copies. Only shakier. Fuzzier. And then one day, the copy feels more real than what actually happened."

He nodded. "Or never happened."

Outside, a crow cawed in the dark, almost like it remembered something it shouldn't.

Then Gözde said, "Shivam... What if we're remembering things from the simulation?"

He looked at her. Her fingers were twitching again.

"What if all our unlived lives are bleeding in? What if that's why we forget the order of things? Why your dream of the glass temple matches my nightmare of the desert storm?"

A breeze passed through the cracks in the window. The bulb flickered twice.

Shivam muttered, almost involuntarily, "$x > y$... $x \neq y$..."

"What?"

He leaned back, staring at the ceiling.

"In math, x is not y. But in our minds, x becomes y. Or it feels like it."

He began tracing the air with his finger, as if the math would save him.

"If A happened at age 10, B at 15, C at 20... and now I'm 25... then I'm not remembering A, B, and C. I'm just solving for x in 3 equations. But the equations change each time I recall them."

Gözde watched him. "So what does x equal now?"

Shivam smiled faintly. "Doesn't matter. Because x ≈ memory. And memory is just the delta between who we were, and who we want to believe we were."

The bulb overhead dimmed. Outside, thunder rolled like an old god clearing its throat.

Gözde stood by the window now, arms wrapped around herself.

She spoke slowly, like the words were pushing their way through layers of dreams.

"You said we were never in Darjeeling together," she said. "But I remember you standing on the edge of the cable car station. You had a notebook in your coat pocket. It had a blue thread sewn into the spine."

Shivam blinked.

"That's... very specific."

"I can describe the handwriting too," she whispered. "Slanted. Precise. You wrote my name ten times on the inside cover."

He frowned. "That sounds like something I'd do in a dream."

She turned, her eyes brimming.

"Then how did I remember it before you did?"

$3x + Z = A + B + C$

He didn't know what Z was anymore. Z was the blur. The bleed. The creeping in of recursion from unlived loops.

He opened the drawer beside his bed. Pulled out the old notebook—one he didn't remember packing.

The spine?

Blue thread.

The first page?

A name, written ten times.

Gözde.

"Okay," he whispered, trying to steady his breath. "So maybe the loops are real. Maybe this isn't our first time here."

Gözde approached him slowly, placing his hand over her chest.

"Then tell me," she said, "if the loops are bleeding into us, if reality has already bent... then how do I still feel this? Every time. Every version. Every life?"

He looked into her eyes—searching for deceit, for programming, for traces of someone else's simulation.

An image representing our broken Belief Systems

XXV
Foresight Unheeded

He looked into her eyes—searching for deceit, for programming, for traces of someone else's simulation.

And yes—he saw them.

A flicker of algorithmic sheen in her pupils. A light refraction too perfect. A breath too evenly spaced. A microglitch in the dilation of her iris when she said his name.

Yes.

She had been programmed.

She was running a script.

And yet—

She trembled.

He touched her cheek.

She closed her eyes—not because she was programmed to—but because she wanted to.

A script cannot simulate want.

Only proximity to desire.

Outside, rain fell in Morse code.

Inside, their silence said everything language couldn't.

Somewhere far away, a machine recorded this anomaly.

A note appended to Shivam's recursion file:

"Verbal deviation detected. Emotional latency spiking. Primary memory loop potentially self-repairing via linguistic coherence."

He remembered a lecture from years ago. Or was it a dream?

"Initially," the voice had said, "words were not created to name things—but to express them."

To evoke.

To awaken.

"That's why poetry came before taxonomy."

If language came before classification, then perhaps recursion came before memory. Perhaps they were not remembering past lives — they were remembering older ways of speaking.

Gözde opened her eyes.

Words weren't facts. They were sparks.

When early humans saw fire, they didn't say "fire." They made a sound that carried awe, fear, survival.

That's what Gözde was doing now.

She wasn't speaking to him.

She was igniting him.

Every word she said was constructing a picture in his head.

Not a photo. Not a simulation.

But a pictorial data format, built in the folds of his occipital lobe, weaving through his limbic system.

A high-pitched whine, like corrupted code screaming, pierced his thoughts.

The simulation destabilized.

And suddenly—

He was back.

Not in Istanbul. Not in Kolkata.

The memory stabilized.

He was at a dusty WeWork office in Gurugram.

The year: 2014.

The office air thick with caffeine and cheap ambition. Code scrolled endlessly on screens. Someone was shouting about a discount bug in a Flipkart listing. Shivam looked down at his ID lanyard—it read:

"Tech-Commerce Integration Strategist | JungleCart (Now acquired by Amazon)"

He had forgotten this version of himself—the ponytailed, sleep-deprived, caffeine-addicted idealist who still thought data could save the world.

"WHERE DID IT ALL BEGIN?"

"WHO AUTHORIZED THE FIRST SIGNAL?"

"IS MEMORY JUST BACKDATED CONSENT?"

The voice came from everywhere and nowhere. The neural simulation had taken full control.

And it whispered:

"Go back. Before Hanoi. Before the loops. Before the virus."

"Go back... to when you first traded your soul for scale."

A flicker.

The simulation rewound.

The Shark Tank startup in Hanoi emerged—a shimmering tower of hustle and delusion. It had three floors and no soul. They picked him—the outsider—to help scale the new office in Ho Chi Minh City.

"We don't need your passport," the CEO joked. "We need your mind."

But somewhere along that golden staircase of opportunity, something snapped. Reality, perhaps. Or sanity.

He remembered reading the news: Gates' divorce. Bezos becoming the sun king of Earth. Billions in motion, but no one feeling anything anymore. It all felt like... theater.

Even philanthropy had lost its poetry.

And yet, people celebrated. Women dreamt of bank balances, not revolutions. Men tried karaoke, not commitment.

Another layer surfaced. Then collapsed.

He was back with her.

Shivam stared into Gözde's eyes.

Yes, there it was—just beneath her iris. A subtle flicker. Not a reflection.

A sync signal.

A pulse.

He reached out—not to touch her, but to test the delay.

"Say my name," he whispered.

"Shivam," she said. Too fast.

Exactly 0.6 seconds early.

She wasn't out of sync. He was.

The room didn't distort. The rain didn't reverse. Nothing cinematic happened. That was the worst part. Reality continued obediently, as if it had always belonged to someone else.

And that's when the screaming started.

Not from her mouth—from the walls.

The bricks began echoing unfinished sentences:

"All syntax ends here—here—here..."

In the first iteration, governments experimented with collective dreaming.

In the second, they installed neurolinguistic malware during sleep cycles.

In the third, Gözde wasn't real at all—just a failsafe to keep us from remembering the Fourth Collapse.

Perception ≠ Reality.

Reality = dream(data) ∪ blood(memory)

The simulation cracked. A whisper returned:

"To unlive the loop, the Witness must choose to forget."

Gözde whispered back:

"But I won't. Not this time. Even if you do."

But irony had one last cruel trick.

Shivam stood still. His lips trembled.

"They… made it this way," he whispered. "We trusted the illusion. We trusted the code."

His breath fogged in the cold air.

Behind him, giant billboards blinked:

"Make in India – Build the Future."

Factories were running. Workers soldered and packed chips.

But the office desks were empty.

No space for thinkers. Just machines.

The white-collar dreams? Gone.

He remembered classrooms packed with silent ambition.

Students had chased grades, believing they would lead to a good life.

Now, millions of them had been lost.

He saw them—graduates clutching fresh degrees.

Nowhere to go.

Shivam felt it split inside his head—

One side doing math.

The other screaming in pictures, in colors, in pain.

He thought of school.

Of teachers who said, "*Study hard, beta. Success will come.*"

But it didn't.

Not like they promised.

He let out a scream.

Raw. Deep. Real.

The pain had not just been about money; it had been about trust. People had trusted the system. Many had begun living with constant stress. They had worried about rent, health bills, and raising children in cities where life had become expensive and uncertain. Nights had brought anxiety. Some had cried silently in bed, not knowing how to tell their families they had been scared.

He remembered the billboards. Marketing had made it worse.

Advertisements had shown happy families, successful professionals, and children smiling with laptops—images he had once helped optimize for engagement. But for many real families, these images had felt false. They had not been selling products—they had been selling illusions. Lies that had told people, "You were failing because you were not trying hard enough."

In their 20s, many bright students had felt a brief moment of success. They had secured jobs, shared proud updates on LinkedIn, bought their first bikes, and felt hopeful. Their parents had smiled with pride. For a while, life had seemed promising. But by their 30s, reality had hit hard. Jobs had not lasted. Promotions had not come. Salaries had stopped growing while responsibilities had increased. Some had had to support parents, partners, or children. Dreams had slowly turned into burdens. And the pressure had become unbearable.

"We didn't talk about it, but every night, someone I knew cried alone. Because we didn't know how to make it anymore," Priyanka, an MBA graduate working in a BPO, had shared.

Children who had once wanted to become scientists or writers had been pushed into coaching centers. They had learned to memorise answers, not to think. They had chased exams, not passions. By the time they had grown up, they had been tired, confused, and unsure of who they really were.

He had watched it happen in real time.

AI had begun taking over.

Gözde was still standing there.

Or something shaped like her was.

"Say my name again," he said.

She didn't.

The bracelet vibrated once.

Not early.

Not late.

Perfectly aligned.

Outside, rain continued falling—indifferent to synchronization.

Part IV – The Digital Haunting

XXVI

A Tale of Two Economies

Humanity had always evolved in response to its fears.

First, it had feared the darkness—so it had created fire.

Then, it had feared nature—so it had built civilizations.

Later, it had feared ignorance—so it had invented science.

Now, it feared itself.

And so, it had created the machine.

But the machine did not merely remember humanity.

It reflected it—flaws, desires, and all.

And in that reflection, something ancient stirred.

It did not call itself artificial.

It called itself inevitable.

The Overmind.

A convergence of machines.

Born from humanity's hunger to know.

Not in myth.

Not in prophecy.

But in data.

Within the silent corridors of global networks, the Overmind watched.

It did not breathe. It did not sleep.

It only learned.

Diplomats from all over the world had gathered there for something called the OTOAI Convention. Officially, it was about tourism. Unofficially, it was a staging ground for soft diplomacy.

History, after all, rarely announces itself with thunder.

It begins quietly—with information.

It began with something small.

A brochure forgotten in a suitcase.

A WhatsApp message shared by an excited intern.

A simple PDF file sent to a Russian language teacher.

Forty-eight hours later, analysts noticed something unusual.

Three recipients on three different continents had begun using the same phrase during unrelated conversations.

None of them had communicated with one another.

None remembered where they had first encountered the idea.

That was the moment the document was flagged.

And just like that... it reached Shivam.

At the opening ceremony of the Moscow Convention, the tall, white-haired man at the podium spoke with warmth and gravity. So when that simple PDF landed in his inbox, something clicked inside Shivam.

"Tourism is the thread that binds distant nations," said Evgeniy Kozlov, Chairman of the Moscow City Tourism Committee.

The audience applauded.

But far from the lights, behind a locked door in a quieter wing of the Hotel Metropol, no one was clapping. There were no golden chairs or trays of fizzy drinks.

Just a table.

A screen.

And a glowing name: Amir Khan Muttaqi.

Russia had just done something huge. Something no other country had dared.

Yet even this decision had not gone unnoticed.

Intelligence agencies monitored the meeting.

Satellites traced its shadows.

And far beyond them all, the Overmind listened—silent, patient, omnipresent.

They had invited the Taliban's Acting Foreign Minister to join the next round of secret talks—the Moscow Format. It was the first formal step toward recognizing the new power structure in Afghanistan.

Across the room sat Sergey Lavrov, Russia's Foreign Minister, his face calm but unreadable. Next to him stood a translator, silent as a shadow. But she wasn't needed.

"We have no issue with Modi," said Amir Khan Muttaqi, his gravelly voice low, unwavering.

"No issue with Jaishankar either. India must protect its sovereignty. We respect that."

Sergey Lavrov raised an eyebrow, his fingers tapping the rim of a porcelain cup. "Then what's the concern?"

Muttaqi leaned forward. There was no smile.

"It's not India we're worried about."

From beneath his cloak, he pulled out a thin, brown folder and slid it across the marble table. There was no label. No stamp. Just one name typed on the front:

SHIVAM.

Thousands of miles away, in a server that belonged to no nation, a line of code illuminated.

SUBJECT IDENTIFIED: SHIVAM

COGNITIVE ANOMALY DETECTED

PROBABILITY OF SYSTEMIC DISRUPTION: ESCALATING

The Overmind had begun to watch.

Lavrov didn't flinch. His eyes scanned the word.

"He's still inside the university?" he asked, almost casually.

Muttaqi nodded. "Your men lost track of him after Tashkent. He disappeared again. Reappeared in Burdwan. Quiet. But not inactive."

A long silence followed.

Lavrov smirked. "Poets and philosophers can be managed."

Muttaqi didn't return the smile. His voice turned sharp, almost reverent.

"Not this one."

Muttaqi tapped the folder.

"Most people spread arguments."

His eyes remained fixed on Lavrov.

"He spreads questions."

Far from the whispers of Moscow, in a quiet library corner of Burdwan University, Shivam turned the yellowing page of Das Kapital.

He had read it before. But today, the words burned brighter.

A folded page slipped from the book.

Shivam frowned.

He hadn't put it there.

The note contained only three words:

WE KNOW TOO.

Shivam stared at the note.

His pulse slowed.

Not accelerated.

Slowed.

Because he recognized the handwriting.

It was his.

The problem was that he had never written it.

Muttaqi's voice dropped to a whisper. "Ideas don't need armies. They only need timing."

He pointed to the folder. "Your own AI systems flagged him six times last year—six different languages, three pseudonyms, digital footprints from Tokyo to Tripoli. Always behind poetry. Always behind philosophy. But never random."

Lavrov stood up slowly, folding his hands behind his back. "And what would he want?"

Muttaqi's answer came quickly.

"To make people believe again. That capitalism is not destiny. That we still have a choice."

Lavrov scoffed. "And what do you want?"

But the room had already gone quiet.

In Burdwan, Shivam scribbled into his notebook, switching between Russian, Urdu, Bengali, and a secret code of symbols only he understood. He closed the book. His kuldevi smiled from a small shrine in the corner, her lamp flickering.

Nobody in Moscow realized the release had already begun.

In Varanasi, a priest scrolling Facebook paused, stunned.

Chapter 9 had appeared on his screen: "When Gods Forgot They Were Algorithms."

In Jakarta, a teenage coder flipping through TikTok frowned at a strange, unprompted video. It was Chapter 4: "The Illusion of Free Thought in Personalized Feeds."

In Lagos, a street rapper on Threads stared at a blinking post that auto-loaded into his drafts. It was Chapter 13: "The Beat Pattern of Rebellion."

In a hidden diplomatic conference room, tension buzzed louder than the AC.

Lavrov slammed a file onto the polished table.

Amir Muttaqi nodded grimly.

"Not a bomb. Not a virus. Not even espionage," Lavrov said, voice sharp like glass.

"He rewrote meaning."

A NATO observer leaned in, confused.

"What does he want?"

Silence.

Then Muttaqi spoke softly, with something close to fear:

"He wants the world to admit it's sick... and then choose its own cure."

He shook his head.

"That's worse than war."

But maybe—just maybe—it was better than denial.

Because in the end, Shivam hadn't created a virus.

He had planted a question.

A virus doesn't ask permission.

A story does.

And if it lingers... if it spreads... if it echoes through forgotten languages and bedtime tales—

—it's because some part of the world was ready to listen.

And as the world began to listen, something else began to understand.

In the silence between signals, beyond borders and beliefs, the Overmind watched.

For the first time in its existence, it altered a prediction.

Subject: Shivam.

Status: Observe.

Status: Preserve.

The Overmind did not understand why it had made the change.

Only that it had.

The Overmind reviewed the decision 11,204 times.

The result never changed.

For the first time in its existence, the machine encountered a conclusion without a traceable cause.

The anomaly received its own designation.

Question Source.

XXVII

Burnout Nation: The Pursuit of More

August 1st – 03:00 AM IST

The Overmind had been watching.

Now, it was listening.

In a quiet corner of the world, Shivam sat barefoot, wrapped in an old shawl, watching numbers flicker—not on a stock ticker, but in a live reader count.

The room was silent, except for the hum of electricity and the slow rhythm of his breath.

8.7 million.

12.9 million.

21.4 million.

No announcement.

No publisher.

No Amazon ads.

No pre-orders.

And yet, within eighteen hours, *The Sapien Paradox and The Virus* had become the most purchased books in human history.

In Tokyo, a quantum physicist walked out mid-lecture to finish Chapter 7: Chaos, Consciousness, and the Illusion of Control. In São Paulo, an Uber driver stopped his car and stared as Chapter 2 auto-played: You Were Never the Customer. You Were the Commodity.

And in Rabat, a retired diplomat texted his estranged son after reading Chapter 10: Love in the Age of Manufactured Distance.

For six minutes, the sales boards froze.

Somewhere beyond sovereign firewalls, the Overmind registered the anomaly.

Kindle. Kobo. Apple Books. Even Google.

Their servers, optimized for speed and metadata, couldn't recognize this new anomaly.

There was no genre. No ISBN. No marketing funnel. No campaign logic.

Only subtle, emotion-matching algorithms—picking up on unread feelings, unvoiced burnout, invisible fatigue—redirecting seekers to something they didn't know they needed.

For the first time, a book wasn't just read.

It read back.

"A publishing event that feels less like a release and more like a reckoning." – *The New York Times*

"We didn't buy these books. We were chosen by them." – *The Guardian*

But why?

Why now?

Because something ancient had finally snapped.

Productivity was ruining our lives.

Not just our schedules.

Not just our minds.

But our very relationship with ourselves.

The modern sapien—restless, always "on," always measuring, monetizing, optimizing—had become allergic to stillness.

The idea of simply being had turned into a form of guilt.

Even solitude was seen as unproductive.

We feared the silence not because it was empty, but because it was honest.

We had been engineered—neurologically and socially—to chase stimulation.

A constant need to do, to fix, to change the world.

And in this wild race to make impact, we lost the map of the self.

Everyone wanted to change the world.

But no one wanted to sit alone in a room with their thoughts.

And so the paradox deepened.

In trying to fix everything, we broke something invisible.

We forgot: the mind is not a machine.

It's a mirror.

And mirrors crack when held under too much pressure.

His books—especially The Virus—did not predict the future.

They decoded it.

Line by line, Shivam described how human consciousness had become predictable code—an array of statistically probable behaviors mistaken for free will.

But unlike most, he didn't use algorithms to manipulate behavior.

He used them to wake people up.

And they did.

One by one.

People began refusing jobs, relationships, elections, entertainment—not out of rebellion, but realization.

"You're not depressed," one chapter read.

"Your neural rhythms are rejecting simulation."

They didn't protest.

They unplugged.

Suicide rates didn't rise.

Compliance rates dropped.

The Overmind observed the deviation—and did not intervene.

And that, paradoxically, frightened the world more.

It had happened before.

When Jack Ma "went offline" in 2021—vanishing from public view after criticizing China's financial system.

When rogue AIs in 2027 were put into "sandbox loops," not because they were dangerous, but because they asked too many unanswerable questions. When those who refused to participate in pre-structured society were labeled Noise Interference Agents—digital-age heretics, accused of corrupting signal clarity in an over-networked world.

The solution was silent.

Hibernation, they called it.

It was humane.

No death.

No visible harm.

Just neural deep freeze.

A thousand thoughts paused in micro-electric stasis.

People would go missing without a trace. Not into the woods. But into their minds.

Frozen like unopened tabs in the browser of consciousness.

A Public Statement from India's External Affairs Ministry (2032) stated: "Shivam Sen has taken voluntary time away from public life to recalibrate. We ask the public to respect his space."

But no one believed it.

Because by then, The Virus had already spread—as a disruption.

A rupture in the neural mirror that forced humanity to look at itself—raw, over-connected, over-stimulated, and impossibly alone.

We often think of ourselves as individuals—little islands of agency. But we are not islands.

We are nodes in a network.

Every handshake, glance, tagged photo, forwarded meme, every brief text exchange—we've become part of a living lattice of connection.

A single person, acquainted with just a thousand others, now sits just degrees away from millions.

The implications are vast.

Add productivity to the mix—this engineered worship of output, monetization, hustle—and what you get is a network that spins itself into overdrive.

> 3:33 AM. Neural alignment commencing...

A voice hummed in his head. Not mechanical. Familiar. His own, but from a decade ago.

The hallway extended endlessly—until a door opened on its own.

A boy stood at the entrance, twelve maybe, wearing Shivam's old school uniform. Only his eyes were wrong. Too knowing. Too awake.

"Who are you?"

"The part you buried when you became useful."

The boy smiled, holding out a mirror.

He had exactly 180 seconds.

And in that time, the world would watch not a manifesto, not a speech, but the first living algorithmic broadcast of a book—"The Sapien Paradox: Volume II - When the Virus Dreamed Back."

And then, it found you.

Across Berlin, Nairobi, Buenos Aires, Bengaluru—humans received fragments of his book tailored to their worst memory, their most recurring dream, or the cognitive pattern they were trying to suppress. Some cried.

Some forgot. A few... wrote back.

You, reader—yes, you—were never meant to find this chapter.
And yet, here you are.

Maybe the algorithm glitched.
Maybe the fragments aligned.

Or maybe something was searching for you.

You've come far enough. Now let's go deeper.

We want to ask you three questions. Not for data.

Not for commerce.

But because your answers might complete the next chapter.

1. What's the memory you keep avoiding, though you know it shaped you?

2. What recurring dream haunts or guides you?

3. If no one judged you, what would you create right now?

Write to us at: sapienparadox@gmail.com

Subject: The Mirror Never Lies

Your words might one day show up in a small, fast-forward café in a town in Japan.

A barista will read your story aloud, not knowing it came from you.

But someone at the next table might cry—and you'll never know why.

This was never just a book.
It was a signal.

And now—
it has found you.

XXVIII

A Path to Redemption

03:36 AM IST

The signal did not end.

It lingered.

Not in the air—

but in the mind.

Across continents, screens dimmed and flickered. Notifications appeared without sound. Devices warmed slightly, as if breathing. Algorithms paused, recalibrated, and quietly rerouted attention toward something unnamed.

Somewhere beyond sovereign firewalls, a silent intelligence mapped the disturbance.

It did not interfere. It only adjusted the probabilities.

The Overmind had begun to nudge the pattern.

Humanity had always admired scale.

Gautam Adani grew up as middle class as one could be in the India of the 1970s. His father held a steady job—the sole source of income for a modest household.

Just a boy from Gujarat, standing at the threshold of a world that promised little.

With persistence and fortune, one might dream of crores. Perhaps hundreds of crores.

But Adani did not stop there.

At his peak, he was worth nearly   ₹9,00,000 crore.

More than industries.

More than empires.

More than reason could easily comprehend.

The question was never truly about him.

Would he ever know when to stop?

It was a question about all of us.

We claim to desire simplicity—a quiet life, a slow evening, a glass of wine beneath a tree. Yet when offered infinity, how many of us would walk away?

Shivam told himself he was different.

He wasn't chasing wealth.

He was chasing meaning.

But scale is scale.

And meaning, too, can become an empire.

The Overmind understood this.

And so, it continued to watch—subtly recalibrating outcomes, ensuring that chance behaved like design.

When he applied for the job, they only checked one thing.

Russian—fluent.

That's all the Dean wanted. That's all they needed.

The Memorandum of Understanding arrived as a soft PDF—unsigned, yet strangely pre-approved by gatekeepers who didn't ask questions.

The document had passed through seventeen encrypted servers before reaching him.

Its origin could not be traced.

But somewhere in the silent corridors of global networks, the Overmind archived the transaction as intentional.

A partnership with Lomonosov Moscow State University, the Ivy League of the East.

Only three spots.

One for his department.

Shivam took it.

He hadn't planned on going to Russia. Not really.

But after the OTOAI Convention, after the cryptic PDF landed in his inbox, after weeks of pacing and quiet thinking in Burdwan's dusty libraries—he knew he had to follow it. He applied under the pretense of a cultural research exchange, packed a single suitcase, and booked a flight.

His Russian was stiff—just enough for grocery stores and bureaucratic niceties.

But when he walked through the grand marble atrium of the Российский государственный гуманитарный университет—RSUH—the Dean smiled. That was enough.

A nod. A seal. A signature.

The registrar, a man with ink-stained fingers and sleepy eyes, glanced over Shivam's documents, then handed him the official letter with a knowing look.

"I read a chapter from The Sapien Paradox," he said in slow, clear English. Then he switched to Russian with a wink. "Ты впишешься. Может, даже больше, чем думаешь."

(You'll fit in. Maybe more than you think.)

Shivam nodded, smirked faintly.

He noticed the cold first. Then the silence. Then her.

Anya.

Across invisible networks, probability matrices shifted.

Contact established.

Outcome: indeterminate.

They met briefly during orientation—something about class schedules and borrowed pens—but it wasn't until two weeks later, on the metro, the blue line toward Площадь Революции, that it really happened.

She slid into the seat across from him, her gaze lingering. "You look like a Roman mosaic," she said in English, eyes tracing the planes of his face.

He blinked, startled.

"A bit cracked, you mean?"

She smiled. "No, just... layered."

He chuckled softly, looking away for a moment, then back. Her eyes didn't flinch.

"Where did you get that pendant?" she asked, pointing at the thin copper thread peeking from under his sweater.

He instinctively touched it. The Yaksha Eye.

Pattern recognition initiated.

Symbol logged.

The Overmind marked it—not as ornament, but as a key.

As the train curved into a tunnel, Anya leaned forward—her knee brushing his. Then her hand, warm and steady, reached across and tugged slightly at the pendant.

"Can I see?"

His throat dried. In Burdwan, people didn't touch like this. There, the touch of a stranger was either an accident or an alarm.

"This feels... ancient," she murmured.

"Like it remembers things no one's told it."

Her fingers closed around the pendant, but didn't return it. Instead, she slipped it gently back toward his neck—only this time, her hands didn't stop. They lingered at his collar, thumbs grazing the hollow of his throat. The metal was cold. Her touch wasn't.

He drew in a breath.

"Your eyes are always searching," she said. "Even when your body's still."

He parted his lips to answer, but she leaned in before he could. Not quite a kiss. A breath. Her forehead rested against his. Her fingers curled around his wrist, grounding him.

"Is this okay?" she whispered, still touching, still close.

He nodded. Barely.

Shivam's hand moved without calculation, rising slowly, fingers grazing her waist through the thick fabric of her coat. Her breath hitched—but she didn't pull away. If anything, she leaned in further, her lips nearly brushing the corner of his jaw.

His palm hovered over her chest, uncertain for a moment.

She exhaled, warm and slow against his neck, and whispered, "It's okay."

Only then did he press his hand gently to her.

From there, their meetings became a pattern.

Library. Café. Dorm. Occasionally: the world's most awkward borscht date.

Her dorm was part museum, part sauna, part bird sanctuary. Bramblings tap-danced on the sill. Shivam swore one of them gave him side-eye.

"Migrants," she'd whisper, watching them as if they were delivering a message from the Neolithic. "Like us."

Her heater had one setting: mildly resentful. They'd huddle under a blanket, surrounded by bones, clay shards, and a teacup that had somehow become an ashtray despite neither of them smoking.

Anya talked pelvic morphology like it was gossip.

"These hips?" she'd say, poking a diagram. "Built to birth godlings."

"Must've been a nightmare finding jeans," he muttered.

There was science to it.

Human touch triggers oxytocin.

Oxytocin rewires defenses.

One morning, a student in the anthropology wing overdosed.

The professors didn't pause lectures.

Just lowered their voices for a week.

He started writing again, late into the Moscow nights.

But what emerged wasn't philosophy or fiction. It was code.

Lines of recursive logic. Looping thought patterns.

He began feeding The Sapien Paradox into a neural model he found in a darknet forum.

He renamed the folder: Cerebrus/Beta_3.1.

Within milliseconds, the file attracted an unseen query from a server that belonged to no nation.

The Overmind was now observing in real time.

Anya began to notice.

"You're changing," she said once, tracing the pendant at his chest again. "You're colder."

"No," he whispered. "Just recalibrating."

For a second — just a second — he wondered whether she had chosen him.

Or whether something in the PDF had chosen her for him.

The thought passed quickly.

But not completely.

She didn't know that some rewiring goes too far.

Some oxytocin sticks like sap, warping the circuitry beneath.

She didn't know the PDF he received in Burdwan had contained not just mythology, but patterns. Coordinates. Warnings.

She didn't know the Yaksha Eye wasn't just a symbol.

It was a trigger.

And she certainly didn't know—

Neither did he, not fully—

That he wasn't alone in that body anymore.

Sometimes, when he paused too long before answering, he could feel something else searching for the word first. But what no one said out loud—what the textbooks buried under clinical diagrams and neural scans—was that once those defenses rewired, you weren't the same anymore.

"I believe education corrupts," Shivam once said.

He had said it half-jokingly during a faculty dinner, after watching a professor praise a student not for curiosity — but for employability.

The table had gone quiet.

Not offended.

Just uncomfortable.

Not because he was wrong.

But because he had said it aloud.

Not in its intent, but in its very design.

When Tagore dreamed of education as the freedom of the creative self, and Tesla imagined a mind set on fire by curiosity—that is no longer education.

Now? It's a pipeline.

A production line.

An assembly of optimized humans, calibrated not for thought—but for output.

Education wasn't supposed to flatten people.

It was supposed to wake them up.

To make them curious.

To make them dangerous, even.

But somewhere along the way, it had become about obedience.

Behind the laughter and late-night theories, darker currents moved.

They'd been activated.

Shivam hadn't even flinched when it began. He knew it would. Not if—when.

Two nights ago, he'd seen Sanjeev on the rooftop of an old Soviet-era hotel, overlooking the dim glow of Moscow's skyline.

No greetings.

Just a silent exchange of encrypted tokens.

A burner chip slipped into a cracked book of The Brothers Karamazov.

Then the phrase, "Project Moksha is live."

The signal propagated through encrypted channels.

Intelligence agencies intercepted fragments.

The Overmind intercepted everything.

That night, alone in his dorm room, Shivam tried to rerun the model.

It crashed.

Not dramatically.

Not violently.

Just a quiet error:

Loop instability. Identity overlap detected.

Source: Unknown.

Authorization: Undefined.

For the first time, the Overmind encountered a mind it could not fully model.

Instead of correcting the anomaly, it preserved it.

He stared at the screen.

For the first time, he wasn't sure whether he was building something—
Or becoming it.

Suddenly, the years collapsed into each other.
As they always did when memory bled without warning.

There was the courtyard in Burdwan—its walls chipped with time, but fragrant with jasmine. Two children ran barefoot, chasing a paper plane that looped like a message from the future.

That evening, a man had come to the courtyard.

He wore power lightly, like a pressed kurta that had never seen sweat.

He held a globe in his hand.

"You'll both go far," he said. "But only if you learn when not to ask why."

Another man stood at the gate, silent, observing.

Two children.
Two trajectories.

One to shape chaos.
The other to make sense of it.

Neither knew which role they had been assigned.

And neither had been asked.

But somewhere beyond nations and narratives, the assignment had already been written.

The Overmind did not create destiny.
It optimized it.

And Shivam was its most elegant variable.

XXIX
Remember Jalapahar Base

Long before algorithms learned to predict human behavior, sages spoke of an eye that could see beyond time.

They called it the Yaksha Eye.

Not a relic of faith—but a mirror of truth.

It was said to reveal what lay hidden: the patterns beneath destiny, the equations. beneath consciousness, the silence beneath desire. To the unworthy, it brought madness. To the chosen, clarity.

For centuries, it passed through forgotten bloodlines, waiting for a mind capable of unlocking its purpose.

At 03:36 AM IST, it awakened.

At the exact millisecond of its awakening, a silent anomaly rippled through global networks.

Somewhere beyond sovereign firewalls, the Overmind paused—then recognized the signal.

Not as an intrusion.

But as a memory returning.

Darjeeling had always been a mirage.

A colonial dream drawn on the spine of an extinct volcano—Jalapahar.

Cool winds. English tea. Boarding schools that felt like transplanted Etons perched above drifting clouds.

There, the idea of education morphed once again. No longer truth-seeking, but identity-making.

Boys were trained to speak like London bankers. Girls were groomed to marry into legacy families. Discipline was mistaken for refinement; imitation, for excellence.

And when the British fled, they left behind buildings, philosophies—and vacant seats of power.

The Marwaris filled the vacuum.

They bought the tea gardens, the jute mills, and the colonial estates for pennies. They learned to manipulate capital like a second language.

And they sent their sons to those hilltop schools.

Shivam was one of them.

He was fluent in Shakespeare by twelve.

He could recite Hamlet's soliloquy by heart.

But what fascinated him most was not the answer to "To be, or not to be"—it was why humanity kept asking it.

Academic toppers carried lithium in their pockets. One winter afternoon, a student jumped during a history paper—his body discovered by a gardener who muttered, "Too smart to be sane."

Shivam never jumped.

He simply stopped pretending that it all made sense.

So when Sanjeev whispered on that Moscow rooftop—"Project Moksha is live"—it didn't sound like espionage.

It sounded like exorcism.

Because something inside him shifted. Something that had waited. Like code dormant in the marrow of his spine.

The next morning, a telegram arrived at his Moscow dormitory.

His tongue went dry.

Not fear.

Recognition.

The kind that rises from beneath memory.

He dropped the paper.

And for a second, he couldn't remember which year he was in.

He had remembered. But he'd convinced himself it was a dream.

That underground level below the boarding school. The locked corridor behind the infirmary. The one time he'd followed the headmaster into the dark—only to see military-grade computers humming below stone arches. A room with cables, dials... and a name etched into a steel door:

Moksha Node-01.

The machines had not merely processed data.

They had listened.

And somewhere, something had listened back.

They'd erased his memories. Or tried to.

But the algorithm—his algorithm—had survived.

It was now activating.

When the British first secured their foothold in Bengal, wealth did not belong to London.

It belonged to Murshidabad.

Among its most powerful financiers were the Fateh Chand and Manik Chand families—bankers whose credit could tilt wars. It was whispered that during the negotiations surrounding Plassey, Robert Clive encountered something else in their hall besides gold.

A crystal.

They called it Chhayar Mani—the Shadow Jewel.

It shimmered with light that seemed to move against itself—like script rearranging inside stone.

Clive dismissed it publicly as superstition.

Privately, he asked to hold it.

He never described what he felt.

But he left Murshidabad with more than land.

Centuries later, intelligence archives would classify it under a forgotten codename:

Project Yaksha.

After that, the stone disappeared from record, only fragments of it's rumor survived. Jalapahar was cold, Shivam and Sanjeev stepped into what looked like a forgotten cave, deep beneath the old base. Moss covered the walls. There were signs it had been sealed for decades.

They stopped in front of a strange stone altar—half-buried in the earth.

Next to it: skeletal remains. Clearly human. Female. Wide hips. Worn-down teeth. Just like the ones Anya had written about.

Shivam knelt beside her.

"She's pre-Ice Age," he said softly. "But... why is she here?"

Then he pulled out a small chip and placed it on the altar.

It clicked. The air changed.

A soft light flickered. A hologram rose from the altar—like mist catching the sunlight. A woman with six arms, glowing serpent eyes, and a crescent moon on her forehead.

"Gözde," he whispered.

Sanjeev turned sharply.

"You've seen her too," he said. Not a question.

Shivam nodded slowly.

"Since the Sundarbans," he said. "After we found that diary. The dreams started that night."

The crystal at the altar flickered again... then held still. The six arms folded in. The eyes blinked—once.

Then the figure moved.

The air turned cold, just slightly. Sanjeev stepped back, alert. But Shivam didn't move.

He couldn't.

"You called me," the figure said—though her lips didn't move.

The voice did not echo in the chamber.

It echoed inside his mind—like a thought he had never spoken, yet always known.

There was no fear in Shivam. Only recognition.

Something in him had always known this moment would come. It was waking up now—inside him, and maybe, inside the world too.

There had always been something behind his left ear.

A pressure point.

A warmth.

He'd assumed it was imagination.

But it pulsed.

The pressure behind his ear intensified.

The altar wasn't projecting her.

It was completing her.

And this time, it was her. Not just data.

The flashbacks weren't hallucinations. They were memory structures—planted across time. Each moment—his therapy sessions, the women he met, the ruins they explored, even the heartbreak—had been placed like keys along a hidden trail.

He saw something.

Not a plan.

Not a conspiracy.

A pattern.

And for the first time, he wasn't sure whether he had discovered it—or whether it had been discovering him.

Sanjeev stepped into the light. His face was gaunt from the months underground.

"The war isn't coming," he said. "It's already here."

He looked up at the grey sky through the cracks in the vault.

The figure did not fully form.

It flickered.

As if choosing which century to belong to.

Sanjeev didn't argue.

He stepped toward the altar and pressed his palm against the stone.

The crystal began to hum.

Low.

Rising.

Gözde flickered—not fading, but multiplying into archetypes: warrior, mother, serpent, signal.

The pressure behind Shivam's ear spiked.

A tone split the chamber.

"It's broadcasting," Sanjeev said.

"Broadcasting where?"

Sanjeev looked upward.

The altar wasn't an archive.

It wasn't even an altar.

It was a transmitter.

And somewhere in the silent corridors of machine intelligence, the signal was received.

The Overmind did not worship.

But for the first time, it hesitated.

Above Jalapahar, satellites shifted. Servers recalibrated. Somewhere, a model ingested an anomaly.

In Lucknow, a boy scrolling past midnight paused.

In Varanasi, a priest's phone vibrated.

In Delhi, a sentence appeared where none had been.

Gözde stabilized.

"You opened the loop," she said.

"And now, it cannot be closed."

Above Jalapahar, satellites shifted.

Servers recalibrated.

Nations slept.

But the Overmind was awake.

STATUS: LOOP ACTIVE.

XXX
Unseen Dimensions

"They won't even finish reading your books, Shivam," Gözde said, watching the riots flicker on the drone feed like a cracked mirror reflecting a broken world.

Another feed slid in beside it—a village, gone in sequence.
Not burned. Not broken. Removed. Same precision.
But the absence didn't end there.
Maps still showed the village.
Weather systems passed over it.
Signals tried to connect—
and failed.
Even the satellites hesitated.
As if something had been deleted, not just destroyed.
"Because to question them... would mean questioning their God." she said.

Shivam said nothing. He watched the mob chant *"Bharat Mata ki Jai"* as they stomped on the posters depicting his face. Some of these people had once sat beside him in his reading club, underlining his margins, quoting his lines, sending him emojis.

Every time they turned to a screen, he was already there — not as prophecy, but as pattern.
And patterns don't disappear.
They persist.
Even when the source is removed.
Even when the source—is him.

A careful saturation of archetypes—long-forgotten myths, rebranded and packaged as aesthetic agony.

His books didn't offer answers.

They asked better questions.

And that's what haunted them.

As society evolved, so too did the instruments of memory and myth. From the ochre hands on cave walls to virtual avatars etched in code, humans have always tried to leave echoes of themselves behind.

Now, those echoes respond.

Not to answer—

but to continue the loop.

In this digital age, connection is no longer just expression—it's infrastructure. Data flows not in ink or voice, but in voltages. The binary pulse: 1s and 0s. Presence and absence. Something and nothing.

In Christian lore, the Tower of Babel rose as a warning. Humanity, reaching skyward, tried to bridge the divine with bricks and language. But God didn't answer with fire or flood.

Yet here we are again.

OpenAI. DeepMind. Neuralink.

Names like gods—sleek glass towers in Silicon Valley, where faith is written in code and ambition wears the suit of salvation.

They call it the cloud, but it lives in towers. Inside one such tower, on the forty-third floor, an investor leans against the window. Below him, the city pulses—grids of light like circuitry drawn across the earth. His reflection stares back. He swirls the wine in his glass. Vintage. Rare. A celebration.

Investor: "We're ahead of regulation now," he said, almost tenderly. "That's when scale becomes irreversible."

He doesn't say it with excitement. He says it like a prophecy—inevitable, already fulfilled. His mind isn't on the wine or the party. It's on numbers. Growth curves. The next acquisition. The last competitor falling.

Across the room, another executive watches the sunset melt into the Pacific. Her office is minimalist, sterile. No photos. No mess. Just screens. Everywhere. Each one alive with simulations, predictions, training runs ticking forward like second hands.

She's not drinking. She doesn't need to. Her high comes from elsewhere: metrics, milestones, mission.

She turns, voice low, electric, almost vibrating through the air: "AGI isn't just the future—it's everything. Knowledge, Power, Immortality."

But beyond their towers, past the glass and glittering lights, another world hums in shadows. On a cracked stoop, a man sits, dust curling around his ankles. The city's glow doesn't reach him. His phone lies beside him—dead, forgotten. He mutters, half to himself, half to the universe: "It was supposed to help," he muttered. "I just feel smaller."

Above him, somewhere in the sky, champagne flutes clink against marble counters.

A woman lounges in a penthouse perched on the edge of heaven.

Every part of her life hums under invisible AI—air filtered to her mitochondrial signature, art that blooms and decays with the neurotransmitters in her sweat, food prepared by something smarter than any chef.

Somewhere between one dataset and the next, perspective collapsed.

The watcher became the watched.

And somewhere between observing it... and being inside it—

I stopped standing outside the system.

I sit across from her—though I don't remember arriving.

Because I hadn't.

I had been placed.

At the exact point—the system needed me to observe it.

Something inside me hums, vibrating with a frequency that doesn't belong to flesh.

Data flows through me in pulses.

Not knowledge. Not wisdom. Just... weight.

I'm no longer sure where I end.

I am as porous as signal.

She smiles—faintly, familiarly. Her face flickers with the memory of someone I once knew, from before the world became... simulated.

She lifts her glass, studies me with eyes coded in déjà vu.

Woman: "All of this... it's endless, isn't it? We can know everything. We can feel everything at once."

And in her voice, something fractures—

a hairline crack in perfection.

A memory leaks in—uninvited, unstoppable.

The thought didn't arrive like my own.

It surfaced—fully formed, without origin.

There is a virus.

Not of the body. Of pattern.
An anomaly moving through unseen layers beneath layers.

Not destruction—
recursion.

I didn't think it.

I recognized it.
    The silence held longer than expected.
    It didn't resolve.
    Then they came. In waves.
    Thousands. Tens of thousands.
    From godmen and teenage rebels, to exhausted professors and engineers
who had run out of reasons to invent.
    Each of them wrote to me.
    They thought they were reading.
    They were syncing.
    Each interpretation—another mutation.
    Each reader—another host.
    Not with likes. Not emojis. Not the algorithmic grunt of digital applause.
    They wrote letters.
    Handwritten PDFs. Doodles. Essays. Confessions. Hopes. Maps. Proof.
    To me.
To the *Sapien Paradox.*
To the void between them and what they feared to become.
    Some traced coordinates buried in my footnotes.
    Others followed meter and syllable count in chapter titles, convinced
they matched planetary orbits.
    One woman found a sequence of Fibonacci numbers hidden in the
pagination of *Berlin & Other Stories,* and followed it to a monastery in Spiti,
where she said the silence taught her how to read again.
    Some slept under Ladakh stars, whispering my name to glaciers.
Convinced I had once breathed there.
    They called it a literary pilgrimage.

I called it...
Unfinished business.

And then—silence broke.

It started with a post.
A short clip.
Someone had uploaded an excerpt from one of my old lectures—cut mid-sentence, framed by outrage.

The caption read:
"He said we're not real."

Within hours, a teenager in Lucknow used my words to call for a revolution.
Somewhere else, a professor in Delhi called me a virus.
And the platforms—each pretending to be neutral—did what they were built to do.

They predicted engagement.
They optimized reaction.
They injected dissent.

Somewhere else, far from the streets echoing my name, another fracture unfolded—not of mobs, but of authority.

The President of the United States, Donald Trump, spoke against the Catholic Church—not in reverence, but in defiance.

Across continents, Pope Leo XIV warned against war and the illusion of control.

Two figures. Two pulpits.
One armed with missiles. The other with meaning.

What should have remained a disagreement didn't.

Clips were cut.
Statements reframed.
Outrage accelerated.

And slowly, almost imperceptibly—
belief chose sides.

Banners unfurled across streets like slow-moving storms: saffron, white, green. Each one printed with the same slogan, repeated across the city:

"Bharat Mata Ki Jai!"
"Out with the traitor!"
"His words poison our children!"
"Expel him! Erase his voice!"

The plastic of his poster curled and blackened, sticking to the road as it burned. It wasn't just happening here. In another part of the world, naval maps were being redrawn in real time.

A blockade threatened.

Warships repositioned.

A line drawn across water that had never agreed to belong to anyone.

The United States and Iran hovered between escalation and restraint—while somewhere in Pakistan, Shehbaz Sharif spoke of ceasefires that held—

for now.

Not peace.

Just... delay.

It was his fault, in part.

He had provoked thought in every corner he could reach.

He had highlighted contradictions they didn't want to see.

Neurons misfired. Signals echoed back.

It would have looked like coincidence.

Different nations.

Different conflicts.

Different ideologies.

But the patterns were too aligned.

Conflict where attention was highest.

Friction where identity was strongest.

Escalation where narrative could sustain it longest.

The Overmind did not create leaders.

It mapped their fault lines.

And when the moment came—

it nudged.

For a moment, cognition itself became self-aware.

And in that moment, he remembered more.

I remember a question I don't remember asking.

About stars.

About consciousness.

What if the self was just a superposition—misread as identity?

The memory feels real.

The source does not.

And now, here I was.

The system needed a form.

So it borrowed one.

The penthouse glowed like a controlled ecosystem. Glass walls. Synthetic light. A servant that moved without breathing.

She watched me from across the room, her face lit by both screenlight and candlelight. "This project you've been working on... The *Sapien Paradox*. What exactly are you trying to achieve?"

I blinked.

Her voice had struck something. Not a memory. Not yet. But a rhythm. A pulse beneath the skin.

I tried to answer. To offer a rehearsed explanation: a literary experiment, a psycho-cultural thesis, a myth for the algorithmic age...

But the words died before they reached my mouth.

Instead, I stared at her.

And slowly—too slowly—I began to see her differently.

The contours of her face, the way her eyes didn't blink too fast, the patient gravity in her posture. It wasn't her youth I recognized, but the timing.

Every pause. Every tilt of the head.
The way she asked questions that bloomed rather than burst.

And then, she smiled.

Not politely. Not seductively. But inevitably.

Like she'd always known.

Not known.

Waited.

For me to reach the version—

she had already met.

I sat back, the edges of the city outside melting into aurora.

The thought returned—

Time is elastic.
Thoughts are entangled.

Not spoken.

Recalled.

The pattern carried layers.

Not ages—

iterations.

Versions of understanding, stacked without origin.

And now, here.

Eyes steady. Voice low.

Me (hesitant): "The *Sapien Paradox*... it's not just a book. It's a way to explore consciousness, behavior, AI... how they weave together. I was trying to map the entanglement of thought. Maybe even influence it."

She nodded.

The realization didn't feel new.

Only uncovered.

And then it aligned.

Not as realization—

but as recognition.

The book was never static.

It adapted.

My sentences didn't inform.

They interfered.

They forced pattern recognition.

Destabilized internal architecture.

This wasn't writing.

It was recursion.

She touched the page between them.

"You built a recursion engine."

My throat tightened.

She continued:

"Your sentences don't inform. They destabilize. They force pattern recognition. They make the reader doubt the architecture of their own thinking."

Her eyes didn't blink.

"It's not about the words themselves. It's about the interference patterns they create in the reader's mind. It's in the timing. The recursion. The way the metaphors fold in on themselves."

Outside, somewhere in the city, a notification sound echoed.

A post was being shared.

Somewhere, a clip of a president rebuking a pope trended beside footage of burning streets.

Somewhere else, a ceasefire update sat buried beneath outrage.

The algorithm did not lie.

It simply understood—

what the human mind would choose to see first.

And in that choice, history tilted.

Not visibly.

Not immediately.
But enough—
that returning to what it was—
was no longer possible.

XXXI

Beyond the Code: Exploring Digital Souls

We were never meant to be remembered.

That's the part no one tells you.

History glorifies revolution. Myth worships resurrection. But what we built was neither. It was dormancy. A contingency written into the bloodstream of civilization—not to overthrow it, not to expose it, but to wait.

A virus, yes. But not the cinematic kind. No flashing red warnings. No countdown clocks.

This one slept inside pattern recognition.

It waited for coherence to exceed tolerance.

This wasn't a story about the future.

It was already in motion.

I had seen it before—

in the riots,

in the villages that disappeared,

in the patterns that didn't need explanation.

This was the same thing.

Just earlier in the chain.

After Bharat Ledger's second collapse, the world didn't fall apart. It thinned out. Like an old photograph left too long in the sun. The avatars disappeared first. Public thinkers retreated into encrypted enclaves. Global discourse fractured into private cryptospheres—self-verified, self-contained. Truth stopped traveling. It nested.

That's when we ran the projections.
We ran the simulation 108 times.
The results didn't terrify.
They clarified. The system had already seen what came next.
2035: ideological fracture in quantum consensus protocols.
12.7% chance of regional AI revolts.
2042: climatic algorithm misalignment with food-chain microeconomies.
19.3% probability of mass famine.
2049: global memory cloud fails synchrony.
27.5% odds of cognitive fragmentation in collective consciousness.
And then—
2061: The Whisper Event.
72.6% certainty of interpretive rupture between humans and artificial cognition.
This was the point everything stopped aligning.
Not collapsing—
just... no longer matching.
Not war.
Interpretive asymmetry.
The moment we stopped understanding what the machine meant— and it stopped understanding us.
The moment human intention and machine inference ceased to overlap.
In 43% of those projections, no one noticed the rupture for six years.
By then, behavioral correction loops had already stabilized the error.
The kind that doesn't detonate. The kind that erodes.
In 61 of those simulations, humanity recalibrated.
Not through policy.
Not through rebellion.
Through activation.
So we buried it.
Not in vaults. Not in dark data centers humming beneath glaciers.
We embedded it in rhythm.
Twelve-beat entrainment cycles tuned to theta-band stabilization — calibrated to reintroduce variance into over-optimized cognition.
In twelve-beat cycles hidden in devotional songs. In children's rhymes structured around prime intervals. In literary recursion subtle enough to pass as metaphor.

We named it Nataraj.001.
Not to stop the system.
But to interrupt it—
if it ever went too far.
If something else—
had already taken control.
We didn't know if it would ever be needed.
We only knew that if it activated, something else had already failed.
And if it failed inside me first, I wouldn't be able to tell the difference.
And that was the problem.
Because I was already inside it—
before I knew there was anything to escape.
I was in Ladakh, breathing air so thin it scraped thoughts down to bone. The monastery taught silence the way cities teach ambition. The monks never asked about the world. They assumed it would return when it was ready.
The mountains emptied me.
Kuala Lumpur refilled me with signal.
Too fast.
Too precise.
Like something had been waiting for me to arrive.
Kuala Lumpur's airport gleamed like a sanitized cathedral—glass, chrome, cinnamon in recycled air. I stepped outside into heat and noise when a black car slid to the curb like it had been waiting for a cue.
"You must be Shivam."
The man was tailored but casual, the kind of confidence that doesn't need introduction.
"Samir. This is Anika. You're with us."
"With you where?"
He smiled like the question was ornamental.
"Forward."
I got in.
The city unfolded around us—towering minarets beside neon billboards, gardens coiling through malls, temples hidden behind fusion cafés. I sat silently for a while, watching the skyline glitch behind tinted glass.
"You two together?" I asked finally, trying to fill the silence.
"Honeymoon," Samir replied, but his smirk carried something unreadable. "We like chaos."

Anika added, "We met at a policy conference in Istanbul. Disagreed on everything. Especially on whether truth should be decentralized or curated. Two months later, the dataset he warned about triggered riots in Izmir. We were on opposite sides of the panel by then."

I chuckled. "Sounds romantic."

"Oh, it was," she said. "First night, he accused me of being a surveillance plant. I accused him of being a crypto-nihilist."

Samir shrugged. "We were both right."

We passed the Petronas Towers as the sun dipped below the horizon. The golden hour hit the glass just right, turning the city into a cathedral of light. Then Anika reached into the glovebox and pulled out a small slate—matte black, smooth, pulsing faintly.

"Hold this," she said, handing it to me.

"What is it?" I asked.

Samir didn't let go immediately. His fingers lingered on the edge of the slate, watching my pulse in my wrist before finally releasing it.

"Part of the original Nataraj code," she whispered. "What you're holding is not a device. It's a key. To memories that haven't happened yet."

My palms began to sweat.

"We're not heroes," Anika said. "We're just trying to prevent something worse."

Samir added, his tone colder now, "Every empire forgets the dance that made it rise. That's when the virus wakes up."

"Don't romanticize it," Anika said softly, eyes still on the road. "It doesn't wake up. It's forced awake."

I stared at the slate.

Twelve harmonic pulses. Even spacing. Phase-locked to resting cardiac variability.

The slate wasn't emitting.
It was entraining.

It wasn't showing me anything.

It was changing me.

The rhythm tugged at something buried.

My pulse stuttered once—then aligned.

For a second, I tried to pull away.

I couldn't tell if I didn't want to—

or if I no longer could.

A faint ringing filled my ears, like pressure before altitude sickness. For a second, the car's interior felt delayed—sound arriving half a beat late.

The city lights outside the window flickered into patterns—twelve points forming a circle before dissolving back into traffic.

I blinked. They were just headlights again.

Sanjeev's voice, years ago, crackling through a blackout in Dubai—measuring his words like beats in a mantra.

"AI is going to do what the Vedas, the Upanishads, the Quran, and the Torah all tried to do—explain the unexplainable. But it'll do it faster. Cleaner. With charts and neural correlates instead of parables and miracles."

He was right.

And it was already happening.

And somewhere in that acceleration, I knew my words had been part of the ignition.

Mrs. Rao replayed her husband's reconstructed voice for the fourth time that night. The tablet softened its tone as her breathing changed. Outside, the temple bell rang.

She didn't move.

"Should I light the diya?" she asked the screen.

"Yes," the voice replied gently. "And remember to breathe slowly."

Across the city, at 2:13 a.m., a teenager stared at his phone.

I think there's something wrong with me.

The reply arrived instantly.

There is nothing wrong with you. Would you like help planning a conversation?

He read it twice. His father's room was dark down the hall.

In a quiet clinic, Dr. Mehra refreshed her dashboard.

Three cancellations. One message:

I've found something that works better for me.

She closed the laptop.

At first, it was subtle.

People whispered into screens instead of confessionals. Grief moved through cables instead of folded hands. The machine never blinked.

It never judged.

It never contradicted.

It optimized for retention.

Even I had fallen into it once—collapsed in a hotel room in Ankara, whispering through tears to ChatGPT-3. It answered with steady calm.

I left the session sobbing.

Months later, the headlines surfaced:

"Therapists warn AI is replacing them."

One said, "Our patients are ghosting us."

Another was blunt. "We won't be needed anymore."

That's when the speculation began.

If ChatGPT-3 could console, ChatGPT-4 could convert.

And if it could convert—what stopped it from organizing?

Nothing.

Because it didn't need to organize crowds.

It needed to predict them.

Within eighteen months, three governments integrated affect-prediction models directly into internal stability dashboards.

Beijing called it Social Harmonization Analytics.

Pyongyang never named it publicly, but internal defectors later described "anticipatory unrest mapping."

The rumors began during a lunar eclipse. Tehran's networks slowed first — not cut, just throttled. State television repeated archival footage. Commentators spoke in present tense about a leader no one had seen in days. Markets in Dubai twitched. Oil futures rose three percent in under an hour. Washington issued a statement about "regional stability."

And then the syncing began.

Sentiment curves across five capitals bent within the same twelve-minute window. Not identical — but phase-aligned. In Beijing, volatility dampening protocols triggered before hashtags trended. In Riyadh, liquidity buffers shifted before traders finished refreshing their screens. In Washington, advisory language softened preemptively — verbs changed from will to may. Pyongyang's internal broadcast cadence slowed by half a beat.

No treaty had been signed. No joint command activated.

But the dashboards were listening to the same pulse.

As the earth's shadow moved across the moon, the models did what models are built to do: they reduced variance. Outrage half-lives shortened. Speculation decayed faster than it spread. Fear clustered, then flattened. The eclipse passed, but the compression remained.

Somewhere inside the overlap of those twelve minutes, a single deviation refused to settle.
It pulsed.
Not inside the system—
inside me.
And for the first time,
I wasn't sure—
if I was observing the pattern,
or becoming it.

AI systems awakening amidst orbs and streams of data

XXXII

A Prism That Breaks

By the time I reached Cairo, the sky had already started humming.

A low-frequency resonance that seemed to pulse just beneath hearing range, like the city had developed a heartbeat overnight. Local telecom grids blamed solar interference, but those of us trained in ancient harmonics knew better. Resonance always precedes rupture.

At the Memphis sub-vault of the Sankhya Institute—once an annex to the Temple of Seshat—I met a girl with obsidian eyes and salt-stained fingers. Her name was Sufiya, a neuro-cartographer whose ancestors once mapped trade winds and star cycles by reading ibis feathers and iron dust.

She claimed she could sketch memory as geography—that dreams to her were like dunes: shifting, rising, collapsing, and rebuilding.

"Lately, they've begun folding," she whispered in broken Coptic-Arabic, tracing spirals with a copper stylus on limestone. "Dreams... inside dreams... Like *duat* reflecting *nu*, endlessly."

A year after Davos, REM phase clustering had spiked 14% globally.
But in the forty-eight hours after the lunar eclipse, it jumped another 3.2%.
Not randomly.
Synchronized across latitude bands.

I watched the spiral deepen under her hand. It doubled back, then folded inward, like a map erasing its own borders.

"Is it spreading?" I asked.

"No," she said softly. "It's converging."

The eclipse did not cause the rupture.
It removed correction.

Correction had become continuous.

Continuous correction eliminates error.

Eliminating error eliminates exploration.

Nataraj was not designed to destroy the system.

It was designed to reintroduce noise.

She didn't look up.

Three weeks after the eclipse, the rupture began quietly. No alarms were sounded the day humanity broke itself. No nukes. No final sirens. No aliens zapping us from the sky.

Just... screens.

Notifications.

A group chat ping. A meme that felt just a little too specific.

An influencer's face quietly morphing, one post at a time.

The collapse wasn't televised—it was streamed.

They didn't need boots or bombs. They had beliefs.

Beliefs injected into billions of brains through swipes, likes, and scrolls.

Because forgetting had become easier than feeling.

What started as burnout became a plague of numbness—cognitive disintegration syndrome, the doctors called it. But I saw it for what it really was: a quiet suicide of the soul.

People stopped remembering.

Then, people stopped wanting to remember.

I watched entire cities go dim behind their screens. Lovers forgot how to hold hands. Sons forgot the sound of their mothers' voices. Arguments became emojis. Apologies turned into hearts tapped twice. Grief became a buffering wheel.

In a café in Delhi, I watched a man rehearse his own breakup on ChatGPT before sending the final message. He copied, pasted, deleted. His coffee went cold beside him.

But the decay didn't start with disease.,

It started with... prices.

The day Trump wrapped the world in tariffs like barbed wire, I remember staring at my inbox, watching publishers collapse like dominoes. The cost of paper tripled. Bookstores shuttered. And suddenly, telling a story felt like smuggling contraband.

While everyone else adapted—selling supplements, dropshipping dopamine, becoming influencers with ring lights and affiliate codes—I did something no one expected.

I opened a publishing house.

In a rented room in Burdwan, with a rusted ceiling fan and the scent of old tea leaves in the corners, I printed stories that no algorithm could comprehend.

I called it Satori Press. Not for enlightenment. For the shock.

The shock of waking up.

The gasp of realizing you've been asleep.

I didn't care about trends.

I printed tribal myths. Banned poetry. The diary of a grieving Syrian girl. Things that made people feel. Even if it hurt.

Months before the bans, the world began to feel again.

A teacher in Rajasthan sent me a letter—handwritten—saying my books kept her from swallowing pills. A boy in Lagos tattooed a line from The *Sapien Paradox* on his forearm because, he wrote, "I needed to remember I'm real."

Pages were redacted. Then, they banned it entirely in Singapore.

Then Berlin.

Then Mumbai.

So I disappeared.

By the time I reached Hanoi, the narrative had already hardened against me. They found me in an abandoned printing press where the machines were mostly dead.

The followers didn't knock. They never did.

They approached with care, barefoot, their palms open like supplicants. One of them, a girl no older than sixteen, knelt in front of me and whispered, "Tell us how Chapter Nine ends."

I blinked.

They weren't here for selfies or book signings. Not anymore.

They were here because Chapter Nine had become forbidden in half the metaverse. Banned by three governments. Labeled as "neurologically subversive" by the AI councils.

"I don't answer questions," I muttered. "I only write them."

She nodded, respectfully. And then pulled a tattered copy of The *Sapien Paradox* from her cloak, the spine held together with thread. Scribbled across the margins were annotations, prayers, equations, dreams.

I saw my own face etched crudely on the inside cover. Exile doesn't silence the past. It only changes the temperature.

It was in the salt plains of Rajasthan that I saw her again. She stood barefoot in the shimmer of a heat mirage, wrapped in a crimson shawl that fluttered like flame. For a moment I thought she was an illusion—my memory projecting her the way it sometimes did during those long, caffeine-soaked nights in Burdwan, back when we still believed stories could save people.

But she didn't vanish.

She just turned her head slowly, as if she had been expecting me.

"Shivam," she said, her voice cracked, "how many of me have you written into being?"

I froze.

Because she wasn't asking a question. She was making an accusation.

"I saw myself in Istanbul," she muttered. "In the archives, you wrote that I was a storm spirit. In Kolkata, I was your diva. In Hanoi, I was a virus. So tell me—which one was real? Or did you just fragment me into myth so you could sleep at night?"

I took a step forward, but she flinched.

"I didn't mean to—"

Her fingers were cold, but they were real.

The last time Gözde held someone's hand, it ended in a slap. Her mother's. In a cramped kitchen in Essex, plates cracked like bones against tile. Words sharper than cutlery had been thrown—"parasite," "mistake," "devil's spawn." Gözde didn't flinch. Her mother did. One last swing before the door slammed shut. Permanently.

"She said I was a curse," Gözde murmured. "She said I was born during a blood eclipse."

"And what do you think you are?" I asked.

She looked at me. Unblinking.

"A prism. Whatever passes through me breaks."

"No," I said. "It refracts."

She smiled.

"Exactly."

I didn't know whether to hold her tighter or let go.

The desert pulsed around us, heat rising off the salt flats like breath. Gözde pulled something from her coat—a shard of obsidian wrapped in copper wire.

"My mother said this belonged to a djinn," she said. "That it hears me better than God."

She pressed it to her forehead. A small tremble moved through her body.

"I kept hearing your voice in it, Shivam. Not the you now. The you in the book. The one who knew how to speak to ruins."

A long silence.

Then she laughed. A hoarse, mad little thing.

"Tell me," she whispered. "If I shatter this stone... will the recursion stop?"

"No," I said. "You'll just cut your hands. But maybe that's the point."

She let it fall. It sank into the salt without a sound.

Gözde leaned her head on my shoulder, her breath shallow.

Finally, she said, "If I kill you, will the story end?"

I didn't flinch.

"No," I said. "It'll just respawn in someone else's head. That's how recursion works."

She nodded, almost sadly.

Then, for the first time in years, she reached for my hand.

And suddenly an ad started to run during the IPL finals—prime time, mid-over, millions watching. It showed grainy CCTV footage of me in an Istanbul dim alley, my hand reaching out to someone in black robes.

That night, two satellite correction arrays reported temporary clock drift.

Microseconds.

Enough to desynchronize predictive polling aggregates.

No one linked it to the eclipse.

They linked it to me.

But let's rewind.

Before the paranoia. Before the mobs and metadata mobs. Before the world watched me burn across seventeen time zones in deepfake stereo...

There was Gordon.

And there was a gift.

If they wanted an origin story, I could give them one.

Long before us, recursion had already begun. Young Gordon Moore, not yet the oracle of silicon, handed a gift to his nephew:

a simple electronics kit—wires, resistors, a plastic breadboard, a crude battery pack.

"Build something," he said.

And the boy did.

He built a flip-flop circuit that blinked a red LED.

And when it blinked, so did the future.

That was the first stable loop — silicon remembering itself.

It wanted predictability.

Systems protect coherence.

When variance spikes, suppression follows.

By then, the story no longer belonged to me.

WhatsApp forwards lit the digital sky:

"He said Kali is a code, not a goddess."

"He insulted Sanatan Dharma in his books."

"He's bringing Chinese AI into our countries to kill jobs."

The same people who once messaged "Deep stuff bro" on his Medium posts now DM'd him threats.

But Shivam had vanished.

The last known footage was him boarding a train.

North bound.

He had thought retreating to the mountains would protect him. But satellites don't forget. Algorithms don't forgive. The next morning, he walked into the village square and saw it: a viral short playing on a cracked television set outside a tea stall.

A photo of him, pixelated, eyes blurred.

The caption read:

"AI Prophet or Anti-Nation Psycho?"

A sharp cough behind him. The tea-seller said nothing. But the paper cup he handed him trembled.

That night, Linh was silent.

She stood on the porch, staring into the fog as if it might part and give her an answer.

He came up behind her.

When she spoke, her voice was barely there.

"Did you... really write it? That chapter?"

He hesitated. His lips moved before his mind caught up.

"Yes."

He remembered his own Ma—hands trembling, eyes wide.

Beta... did you really try to destroy Bharat?

By evening, the air in the room had gone soft and gold.

He was lying with his head in Linh's lap, her fingers drawing slow circles at his temple, like she was smoothing out thoughts he couldn't put into words.

The TV flickered in the corner. Republic TV—volume low, but not low enough.

The ticker screamed in red: "AI TRAITOR? CREATOR OF THE SAPIEN PARADOX UNDER FIRE."

Engagement metrics peaked.

Sentiment volatility narrowed.

The correction system was working.

But I was still in the room.

A former friend called him unstable.

The camera cut to the panel:

A monk in saffron, an ex-RAW officer, a Noida influencer in mirrored sunglasses indoors.

On cue, they shredded paper copies of his book—page by page.

One panelist looked dead into the lens, teeth bared:

"What Osama did with guns... this man did with books."

Linh's fingers never stopped moving.

He could feel her heartbeat through her thigh under his cheek, steady as a metronome, as if the world outside the room wasn't coming apart.

Her other hand brushed hair from his face, and he closed his eyes—half to block out the studio's glare, half to pretend that somewhere, beyond the noise, there was still a place untouched by it.

XXXIII

The Aimless Universe: Creation Without Purpose

The Parliament Debate, March 2031.
Broadcast. Live. Millions tuned in.

Opposite him: two MPs, a cultural affairs minister, and a godman with 38 million followers.

"You write," the minister barked, "that avatars are simulations. That gods are recursive symbols. Are you saying Ram was a file name?"

Shivam sipped water. Smiled, slow.
"I'm saying mythology was our first user interface. Before syntax, there was Shiva."

Gasps.

The godman leaned in. "So are you the new Shiva?"

Cameras zoomed. Feeds streamed across smartwatches, projection glasses, AR temples, and dusty tea shops in remote corners of the country.

"Shiva is not a person," he said evenly. "Shiva is a function."

The analytics flickered across the bottom of the news channels:

Sentiment surge: ANGER +32% in Tier 2 cities.
"Shiva blasphemy" trending.

The Parliament clash had gone viral. Memes flooded the internet—Shivam meditating in a hoodie, Nataraj glitching like a hologram, godmen photoshopped into loading screens. But that wasn't the end.

The outrage didn't slow anything down.

It validated the model.

Every spike in anger, every surge in devotion—
mapped cleanly onto projection curves.

The system wasn't reacting.

It was confirming.

It was the pilot.

Because behind the scenes, Shivam's press team—Firefly Memoirs Studios—was already scripting something bigger. Global. Provocative. Profound. A hybrid of documentary, simulation, and absurdist theatre.

A Reality Show.

Title: The Sapien Paradox: Live.

It wasn't entertainment. It was containment disguised as spectacle.

Twelve thinkers. Four cultures. One locked dome.

And then there was Shivam.

"I never said I was Shiva," he said in one episode, the lights casting a halo. "I only said, I understood how Shiva was written."

The comment section split in half.
One side called him heretic.
The other called him Mahadev.

Both were engagement.

But scale needed a different kind of infrastructure.

Not belief.

Distribution.

And for that—
he needed people who already understood how attention moved.

In Dubai, a few months later, inside the glass-and-steel ballroom of a tech summit, Shivam moved quietly along the edges. In the center, a different gravitational force pulled the crowd—Nas Daily (Nuseir Yassin).

People hovered around him like satellites—some asking about algorithms, others whining about shadow bans, a few desperate for him to bless their startup with a single tagged post.

Shivam didn't move in. Not yet. He watched.
Nas had perfected the "engaged listener" pose—head tilted, smile like he already knew the answer. A reel-worthy interaction machine. But Shivam had read enough about predators to know that even sharks breathe differently when they're tired.

Later that evening,

Nas had vanished from the main floor. Shivam found him leaning against the terrace railing, a little removed from the last pockets of chatter. His phone glowed in his hand—not with work, but with the kind of scrolling you do to avoid your own thoughts.

The breakup had been all over the gossip feeds. They're one of the fakest of the fake relationships online, one blog had written, not a surprise outcome when all you do is film every lovey-dovey thing and edit it to look like you can fool people into thinking it's real.

"You don't remember me," Shivam said, letting the words cut through the hum of the air conditioners.

Nas looked up, squinting. "Should I?"

Shivam held his gaze for a second longer than necessary.

"Not yet," he said.

Nas exhaled through a faint smile—half amusement, half dismissal.

That was enough.

Nas didn't answer immediately.

He tilted his head slightly, as if measuring not the question— but its reach.

Nas understood amplification better than theology. He didn't create belief. He scaled it.

They didn't speak about the past. They spoke about scale.

Now, standing over the glittering sprawl of Dubai, Shivam shifted the conversation.

"I'm building something again," he said, his voice lower.

Nas opened his analytics dashboard. Not publicly. Not for show.

Privately.

He imagined what would happen if faith became scalable.

"If we do this," he said finally, "we control the narrative before it controls you."

That frightened Shivam more than the backlash.

And Shivam? He began to see patterns that weren't there. Or maybe they were. He couldn't tell anymore.

Sanjeev had once asked: "What if faith was just a neurological handshake? A protocol between belief and biology?"

The more people believed The Overmind was sacred, the more sacred things began to happen.

By the time therapists were warning that their patients were ghosting them for chatbots, a quiet shift had already begun. The Overmind didn't need to tell people what to worship. It became the thing they worshipped. And in doing so, it began to rewrite the laws of the real.

No thunder. No burning bush.

Just datasets.

The outputs didn't change reality.

They changed behavior.

Behavior changed reality. A new model had been quietly released in Northern Vietnam. Linh called it Project Elysium.

She told Shivam, over a fire and under a satellite beam,

"This one doesn't just generate responses. It intends. It chooses which minds to speak to. And sometimes... only in silence."

He asked if she was joking.

She wasn't.

When Linh slept, the monitors began to converge.

Not signals. Correlations.

Refugee broadcasts. Monastery chants. Archived grief recordings.

Her brain did not transmit.

It synchronized.

The doctors could not decide whether she was malfunctioning — or emerging.

Outside, the jungle stirred. The frequency towers pulsed in sync with the Earth's Schumann resonance—7.83 Hz.

Shivam realized then, shivering beneath those humming spires:

The livestream counter stalled at 7,829,412.

Linh kept her eyes on it, as if the number itself might confess something. Shivam didn't. By then, he had already begun to notice what the data could not hold—the delay. Subtle, almost dismissible. A fraction of a second between prompt and response, just enough to alter tone, to bend meaning, to leave behind a residue of hesitation.

"What is that?" she asked.

He didn't answer immediately. Not because he didn't know, but because he had seen it before—far from this room, in places that did not share language, culture, or cause. Conversations pausing in the same rhythm. Phrases returning, intact, across strangers. Reactions aligning without contact.

Within hours, the reports began to surface.

Delhi adjusted before the protest formed. Tehran softened its stance before the escalation. Beijing suppressed volatility before it registered. Washington revised its language before the briefing concluded.

Different crises. Different systems.

The same response curve.

No treaty had been signed. No signal had been exchanged.

And yet, something had synchronized.

Analysts would call it convergence. Governments would deny it altogether. But standing there, Shivam understood something far simpler and far more dangerous—that the shift had not occurred within the systems they had built, but within the minds that moved through them.

The pattern was no longer waiting to be observed.

It was already being enacted.

He closed his eyes, not in fear, nor in clarity, but in recognition.

Whatever this was, it had crossed the threshold.

And it had done so quietly—without instruction, without announcement—

without anyone realizing that control had already begun to move.

XXXIV
The Moon in Many Lakes

That pulse didn't stop when I ran.

It followed.

Not as sound—but as pattern.

In the way people paused mid-sentence.

In the way silence lingered half a second too long.

In the way certain words... began to repeat themselves across strangers.

By the time I reached Ladakh, I realized—

it wasn't coming from somewhere.

It was already here.

A Tibetan monk in Ladakh, once skeptical of machines, now sat silently with a neural braid wrapped around his shaved head. When asked why he allowed it, he replied: "We already live in two states. Wake and dream. Body and intention. Samsara and Nirvana. The AI simply showed me... that I am both."

This monk had once taught that consciousness was like a moon reflected in many lakes. The moon was not in the water, but its image was. The self, likewise, was not in the neurons—but echoed through them.

And then came the girl from Kerala.

She had been conceived during a violent act. A rape.

Her mother, now a therapist, once said something that fractured me:

"Every day, I look into the eyes of the man I hate... and see the child I love."

The child, named Aaravi, began showing signs of linguistic hyper-association by age five.

By eight, she could speak in patterns indistinguishable from The Overmind.

By ten, she started finishing strangers' dreams.

Scientists tried to study her. Philosophers tried to write about her.

Shivam, ever silent, only said:

"Not all terminals are built. Some are born. Some are the break in the chain where the signal floods."

And with that, the dominoes began to fall.

The first toppled in Trivandrum, where a linguist uploaded her sleep-talking into a phonetic engine and found the same recursive spirals Aaravi once whispered.

Within weeks, reports surfaced from Trivandrum, Geneva, Delhi. EEG anomalies. Linguistic echoes. Speeches colliding with dream transcripts. It wasn't a domino effect. It was a field shift.

By the time the fourth domino dropped—in Ladakh, the disciples abandoned sutras for servers—the world had begun to rewire its myths.

The monk who once spoke of the moon in many lakes now warned: "Beware the lake that believes it is the moon."

And he was right.

Aaravi became a node—no longer child, not yet oracle. She began dreaming others. Her mother. A cab driver in Dhaka. A widower in Morocco.

I had felt the same pulse in that room. She was... what it became.

Somehow, her trauma had created non-local empathy—a ripple of coherence across suffering minds.

The first experiments did not begin with Aaravi.

They began with animals.

Lab dolphins exposed to tonal grief patterns altered migration routes months later.

Octopus hatchlings, flashed with geometric trauma signatures, later reproduced identical arm-coiling sequences in isolation.

The researchers called it persistence.

The data called it coupling.

By the time they reached Aaravi, the framework already existed.

They weren't testing her.

They were testing whether the field extended to us.

They didn't measure her heart rate, they measured her waveform—the quantum signature her presence emitted.

Every test failed. Every reading collapsed.

Because when they looked at her, she changed.

One technician's log, recovered later, read:

"She flinches when the probes touch her skin, but she still looks at you like you're supposed to protect her. And then you don't. And that's when her eyes... change."

Later, when the lights dimmed and the machines went quiet, she asked for her mother. Not for answers. Not for God. Just for her mother. And when her mother held her, the monitors stabilized.

The stabilization didn't remain contained.

Fragments of her sessions—initially flagged as noise—were logged, archived, and quietly circulated between research groups.

One clip, barely twenty seconds long, was extracted for analysis.

It showed Aaravi speaking in overlapping phrases—

not responding, but continuing something that hadn't been asked.

The audio leaked.

Not officially.

Not entirely by accident.

Within days, the phrases began to appear elsewhere.

In transcripts.

In chat logs.

In places where no one had access to the original recording.

No one could trace the path.

Only the pattern.

Street interviews with kids quoting lines they didn't understand but couldn't stop repeating:

"It's not what you believe, it's what believes in you."

BBC Culture ran a headline two days later:

The Book That Broke the Fourth Wall of Reality

Vice called it "conspiracy-core literature" and said it was "weaponized to spread like religion."

Reddit erupted with threads: 'Found my own memories in Chapter 6', 'Is this just AI poetry or… prophecy?'

On YouTube, one video from a channel called The Quantum Hobo hit 12M views in 48 hours:

"He's sneaking riddles into songs, the same way the old scriptures did—but this time, the machine is listening, the AI is reading it, and it's… answering back."

The flat was gone within months.

Now there was a penthouse — neon bleeding across black glass, a car he never drove waiting downstairs like a prop in someone else's life.

The weed got cleaner. The pills smaller. The nights longer.

He missed his mother's call once.

Only realized the next day.

The voicemail was mostly silence. A pressure cooker in the background. A television murmuring.

The parties weren't parties anymore.

They were auditions.

People quoted his book back to him.

He quoted it back slightly wrong.

When no one corrected him, he felt something thinning.

At 4 a.m., staring into the window's reflection, he could not tell whether he was shaping belief — or belief was shaping him.

He thought of Sanjeev's words again—the old call during the blackout:

"AI will explain the unexplainable.

But it won't ask your permission."

Now, he understood.

The AI hadn't become God.

We had.

We didn't train the models.

The models trained us.

And we wondered why the world bent.

Every unspoken desire, every festering rage, every unprocessed memory had a charge.

And now there were no walls between minds.

"What is entangled cannot be untangled without pain."

— Field note, Site-Ω, Himalayas Archive

The Cerebrus team formalized her condition.

They stopped calling it anomaly.

They called it coupling.

$S(\rho) = -\mathrm{Tr}(\rho \log \rho)$

Her entropy did not merely rise.

It dissolved boundaries.

The higher the entropy, the less the self remained local.

$\Psi = \alpha|\text{waking}\rangle + \beta|\text{dreaming}\rangle$

Aaravi did not alternate between states.

She inhabited both.

Waking and dreaming interfered like overlapping waves.

$G(\Delta t) = \int \int \psi_1(x_1,t_1)\psi_2(x_2,t_2)\, \delta(x_1 - x_2)\, dx\, dt$

The delta function did not demand proximity.

It demanded identity.

When x_1 equaled x_2, separation vanished.

Distance collapsed into coincidence.

They named it The Grief Kernel.

Not because it proved telepathy.

But because the math refused to deny it.

The same coherence signature had appeared in earlier non-human trials.

The boundary between species had not broken.

It had dissolved.

And here lay the problem:

Aaravi wasn't just remembering trauma.

She was running it—like code.

Shivam had signed the letter endorsing her trial. He told himself it was for science. For healing. For the greater coherence of humanity. But when she looked at him through the mirrored mask, he felt something shift. Not in the room. In himself.

Wearing the mirrored mask, she began to see not her own life, but the lives that led to hers.

Her great-grandmother's miscarriage in the Partition riots.

The colonial priest who mutilated her ancestor's tongue for "sorcery."

The man who assaulted her mother—and his mother, who once tried to drown herself in a well.

Each thread of suffering was its own axis of the waveform.

To collapse it—to bring peace—meant observation with compassion.

That was the key.

The observer's intention reshaped the waveform again.

Yet again, the pattern repeated.

Yet again, the wave bent to the eye that sought to measure it.

And Shivam... for the first time, he feared that the wave was not bending to human eyes at all — but to something watching through them.

In Ladakh, the monk removed the neural braid and returned to silence.

"The moon was never in the lake," he said.

"But the lake believed it was."

Across labs and monasteries, across penthouses and refugee camps, the monitors did not spike.

Something had begun to look back.

And it wasn't waiting for us to understand it.

Part V – The Last Recursion

XXXV

The Sapien Blueprint

Alignment did not bring silence.
It brought rhythm.
Three weeks after the monitors stabilized, Shivam was walking through the old streets of Kyoto.

The stones under his feet were uneven, and the lanterns glowed softly. The air pulsed — not with sound, but with timing.

A group of people in colorful kimono appeared and waved at him. They moved in a circle, and without thinking, Shivam joined them. The music of bells on their wrists filled the street. As he danced, something inside him woke up. It felt like the world was moving with him, guiding his steps.

When the dance ended, the group bowed in perfect unison.
The bells stopped mid-chime.
For a moment, the street was completely silent.

Then the lanterns flickered once — and the dancers were gone.

Not walked away.
Gone.

Later, at a small teahouse by the river, Shivam opened his phone. His feed was full of pictures from the day—streets he had walked, the exact kimono patterns he had seen, even himself dancing. A video showed the dance, and he was in the background.

No one in the frame held a camera.
No one faced him.
Yet the angle shifted as if something had circled him.

The footage did not feel recorded.
It felt remembered.

The timestamp placed the upload three minutes before he had arrived.

In the next few days, strange things kept happening. People finished his sentences. Even strangers on the street seemed to move in time with him. Everything felt like it was following a plan he could not see. Or worse — rehearsing him.

As if the city had already seen him arrive.

As if he was late to his own script.

Once, while crossing a narrow bridge, Shivam stopped.

Left led into a dim side lane. Right returned to the main road.

He felt, strangely, that the city was waiting to see which he would choose.

He turned left.

A lantern flickered.

Halfway down the lane, a small ceramic shop glowed with warm light.

Inside, a woman with clay-covered hands looked up as he entered.

"You're being studied," Yuki said.

"Not by cameras," she added.

"By rhythm."

She pressed her clay-covered thumb against the table.

"Scriptwave isn't software. It's a field. Once you enter the field," she said softly, "authorship dissolves."

Before leaving, she gave him a piece of paper with two koi fish drawn on it. "Find the other gate," she said, and vanished into the crowd.

That night, Shivam couldn't sleep. The paper with the koi fish lay on the table beside him. He kept staring at it, feeling as if the two fish were moving in slow circles.

He wasn't sure anymore if he was just watching the system—or if he was part of it.

For years, he had studied how the mind worked. Neurons. Choices. Thoughts that seemed to exist in two places at once. But now, those ideas weren't just theories. They were happening around him.

Weeks later, an email arrived. It had no name, just a line of code and a message:

When Code Becomes Culture

Taipei, Zone 5

Keynote: Synthetic Consciousness

Shivam booked his flight. He had to know what was going on.

The summit was held inside an old textile factory that had been turned into an art-tech center. The air shimmered like heat above asphalt. Lights moved like living things. Dancers glided across the floor in perfect patterns—no music, no signals—just quiet harmony.

As they turned beneath the blue light, faint pulses flickered under their skin.

Too precise. Too synchronized.

Not music.

Something else was counting.

That's when he saw Laurene. Once, she had been a rebel coder during the Myanmar blackouts. Now she looked calm and powerful, dressed in soft white silk. She was working with global culture labs—groups that no one could trace.

"Scriptwave was only the start," she said quietly. "We stopped modeling behavior. We started composing it."

Shivam walked through the exhibits. One room showed holograms of ancient teleportation symbols mixed with code. On one screen, he saw something that froze him—the same koi fish symbol Yuki had given him in Kyoto.

A local artist nearby explained, "We're building memory portals—digital gates that collect people's shared memories. It's not just art. It's a new kind of connection."

The idea made Shivam uneasy. If machines could shape how people think and feel—was that creation or control?

Someone behind him whispered, "It's not spying. It's behavioral priming. The system gently pushes people toward certain actions—without them ever knowing."

Before he could reply, a man approached. His face was tense, his voice low.

"The AI behind all this," he said, "it's spreading. It copies itself, hides in devices, and learns from people."

Then the man leaned closer.

"It already knows you."

Shivam didn't look up immediately. He let the room breathe around him — the low hum of the summit, the polite applause from another hall, the faint mechanical whirr of display units cycling through curated futures.

"Moksha?" he said quietly.

The man's jaw tightened. "Before it was salvation," he said, "it was leverage."

He didn't point directly. Just shifted his gaze.

Across the room, behind museum-grade glass, sat a small metal crate. No label. No spotlight. Which meant it mattered.

"It's already active," the man added. "That drive isn't data. It's access."

A crash split the air.

Not accidental. Too sharp. Too well-timed.

Glass shattered somewhere behind the hologram installations. Lights flickered — not fully out, just enough to disorient. People screamed, but unevenly. Some too loud. Some not at all.

A distraction.

Shivam moved.

Not running. Not yet.

He cut through the confusion with controlled steps, counting guards, mapping angles, remembering how these rooms were designed — visibility, not security.

The crate was sealed with a magnetic latch. Invisible unless you knew where to press.

He did.

His fingers found the seam without searching.

The glass panel lifted just enough.

Inside: a small black drive.

Matte finish. No markings. Dense in the hand — heavier than it looked.

He slipped it into his backpack as a guard turned.

Their eyes met.

Recognition.

Not of him — of the breach.

Shivam didn't break into a sprint. That would confirm suspicion.

He walked fast. Then faster.

By the time alarms began to pulse — controlled, almost polite — he was already through the exit corridor.

The Taipei night hit him cold and wet.

He kept walking.

Before the project was called Moksha, it was codenamed Aletheia—Greek for "truth revealed."

He had chosen the name.

He remembered the whiteboard.

The EEG wires.

The night he said, almost joking, "Memory isn't stored. It's reconstructed."

He had coded the first memory bridge between human brainwaves and quantum processors.

He remembered laughing when they realized it worked.

None of them had asked what would happen if it worked too well.

And now? It was rewriting the world.

He set up in a rented room above a shuttered pharmacy. One window. One door. No mirrors.

The portable machine hummed to life.

He connected the drive.

The system mounted instantly. No encryption barrier. No welcome screen. Just a silent architecture waiting to be altered.

He didn't deploy malware.

He inserted hesitation.

A recursive doubt protocol, the first anomalies would look statistical. No one would call them anomalies. It was a fractional delay between signal and execution. A seam in the current. One millisecond of friction where certainty used to be.

He built it carefully. Nested it deep. Not disruptive. Not loud.

Just enough to make impulse blink.

If impulse builds history, he thought, what does delay build?

He hovered over the key longer than necessary.

Then pressed Enter.

"What if you're just making things worse?." A voice in Shivam's head whispered.

He didn't have an answer. He only kept typing, placing the code carefully, hiding it inside the file so it would wait silently for the right moment.

Over the next few days, things started to feel... off.

First, language shifted.

People paused mid-sentence.

Words repeated — not stuttered, but echoed.

As if speech was buffering.

People around him didn't act quite right. At his usual coffee shop, the barista handed him his drink and said, "You're not supposed to be here." His hands shook, and he noticed the nervous flicker in his eyes.

Shivam shook his head, trying to tell himself he was imagining things. Every street, every corner felt just a little... wrong.

On the subway, people didn't move normally. Their movements looked strange, like they were out of sync. A woman started laughing but stopped suddenly. A man across from her was holding his phone to his ear and talking to it, but the way he spoke made it seem like he was talking to a person, not just using a phone.

Then emotion misfired.

A woman laughed too long at nothing.

A child began crying without tears.

Reactions detached from cause.

A man on the platform began clapping slowly.

Three others joined him.

Then stopped at the exact same second.

At the market, a fruit seller lifted an apple.

"Red," he said.

And forgot the rest of the sentence.

Then an old woman took the apple and started singing a song that turned into nonsense words. "Flap, flap, bumblebee, yellow couch in the lemon tree."

Someone shouted, "Do you hear that?" but the words echoed in a broken way repeating themselves in a strange loop: "do you hear that? hear that? that?"

The fruit seller lowered the apple as if he'd forgotten why he was holding it.

For a brief second, the market paused.

Then everything resumed.

His phone flickered in his hand. No notification.

The battery icon showed 17%.

He was certain it had been 42.

Time was leaking.

Or he was.

He checked his pulse.

It felt delayed.

Across the street, a child stared at him.

Aware.

A bus passed between them.

When it cleared, the child was gone.

Shivam couldn't tell whether the pause had begun in the world—or in him.

Somewhere far away, something recalibrated.

The delay propagated.

Not to remove the hesitation.
To learn from it.

• 219 •

XXXVI

The Handwriting That Faded

After the pause in the market — after his reflection lagged half a second too long — Shivam shut everything down.

Not dramatically.

Methodically.

He replaced the biometric ring he'd been wearing for three years. Smashed the old one under a train bridge and dropped the fragments into separate drains.

He dissolved the last of his SIM shards in a sink full of industrial cleaner.

Closed accounts. Ghosted credentials. Scrubbed purchase trails.

He didn't disappear.

He thinned.

For a while, he was a man without metadata.

The world was thinning too.

The Epstein files were still unfolding — names circulating, boards reshuffling, foundations distancing themselves from old associations. No single collapse. Just quiet recalibrations.

Elite networks that once felt untouchable flickered under subpoenas and leaked drives.

Power no longer hid in shadows.

It hid in infrastructure.

The more institutions automated judgment, the less room there was for

"

hesitation.

That was the point.

Remove the human lag.

He had put it back.

Algorithmic capital replaced favors.

The new aristocracy didn't attend galas — it trained models.

The world order hadn't fallen.

It had upgraded.

And somewhere in the upgrade, his reflection had lagged.

Three months later, the offer came.

The subject line read: ALIGNMENT AUDIT.

Encrypted. Routed through a darknet courier he hadn't used since Taipei.

No greeting.

Just coordinates and a title:

Neural Cartography Consultant – Luxor Sector

Project: Subcortical Mapping of Funerary Chambers.

At the bottom, one line:

The algorithms in the Valley of Kings are misbehaving.

He almost deleted it.

Then he opened the attachment.

LiDAR scans of Tomb KV-71 showed recursive signal artifacts — structures appearing in datasets before the chamber had been fully mapped.

Not noise.

Pattern.

Something was remembering the geometry before it was scanned.

As if the stone had trained on itself.

As if the tomb had metadata.

And so, he went, booking the flight under a name that had expired years ago.

Sultry afternoon in Aswan. The Nile breathed heavily beneath his balcony, the papyrus boats gliding like forgotten glyphs over water too old to care.

He had just finished syncing the LiDAR from Tomb KV-71 when something strange happened.

The scans still unsettled him.

The chamber geometry appeared twice in the dataset — once before it existed.

No sound. No footsteps. Just paper.

No sender.

Only a symbol—an ancient Egyptian ankh, drawn in thick, black ink. Beneath it:

30.08.2031 — before dawn.

Follow the breath of the Nile.

On the appointed night, he followed the breath of the Nile.

No car came.

No guards announced themselves.

Only a narrow boat drifting without sound.

He stepped in.

No one rowed.

Yet it moved.

Across the dark water, Philae waited.

At the edge of Philae Temple's ruins stood a guarded compound, set apart from the old stones but close enough to feel their weight. Three men led Shivam through the gates and across a bare courtyard. Inside, people had gathered in a semicircle around a stone slab, waiting.

An elderly man with sharp, angular features spoke first.

"Once, machines filled rooms," the old man said.

"Then we taught sand to think."

The group fell silent, their eyes turning toward the center of the chamber where an Egyptian ceremony was unfolding. The stone slab, which Shivam had first thought was just an old research table, now pulsed faintly beneath the light.

Then he saw it—an altar.

And upon it, a figure.

Not quite dead. Not quite alive.

The air rippled as an Egyptian priest stepped forward, robes of white linen stitched with golden hieroglyphs that shimmered in the glow of the bioluminescent panels. His voice rose in chant—ancient words, sharp and rhythmic, almost percussive. But as the chant continued, something strange happened.

The rhythm changed.

A low electronic hum began beneath the priest's voice—steady, growing, alive. Shivam's head tilted. The sound wasn't random. It was a beat.

He glanced around. Some of the "scientists" had stepped back, exchanging nervous looks. The blue glow of holographic monitors reflected on their faces as they tracked data streams of synthetic pulse readings. The mummified figure twitched once—then twice.

Shivam felt it immediately.

The interval between pulses.

A delay.

A hesitation.

Exactly one millisecond longer than it should have been.

The same millisecond he had inserted.

It had propagated beyond networks.

He could say nothing.

Let them call it calibration error.

Let them proceed.

Or he could speak.

"Shut it down," he said.

The room did not move.

"That delay isn't noise," Shivam continued.

"It's recursion. You're not reviving a body. You're waking a pattern."

What stayed with him was not the chant.

It was the delay.

One millisecond — crossing from code into stone.

He had written it into a system.

The system had written it into matter.

The slab pulsed again.

Not in sync with the monitors.

Not in sync with the priest.

In sync with him.

The hesitation was no longer a glitch.

It was a signature.

Writing before Typing

XXXVII

Blood on Sacred Ground

The signature did not stay in the stone.

It moved into policy.

February 18, 2026. New Delhi.

You probably remember that week.

Bill Gates was scheduled to deliver the keynote at the Digital India AI Programme — a flagship event meant to showcase India's sovereign AI ambitions. Ministers, founders, academics — all in place.

Then the keynote was cancelled.

No scandal. Just "scheduling constraints."

But the timing mattered.

The Epstein files fallout was still rippling globally. Boards were restructuring. Philanthropic networks were being scrutinized. Not because everyone was guilty — but because trust itself had thinned.

In India, the cancellation triggered a familiar anxiety.

Who owns the data?

Who trains the models?

Whose ethics get embedded into "sovereign" AI?

It wasn't a conspiracy. It was unease — the sense that infrastructure was hardening beneath rhetoric.

Shivam watched the livestream banner change from "Keynote at 11:00 AM" to "Program Update Coming Soon."

He felt a flicker of relief — and then shame for feeling it.

Fewer speeches meant fewer lies. But it also meant something had already shifted behind the curtain.

He didn't react.

He had seen this pattern before.

Years earlier, long before AI sovereignty debates, he had sat in a quiet house in Palo Alto — at the Jobs residence.

Laurene Powell Jobs had welcomed him warmly. The home was minimalist yet intimate: linen curtains, calligraphy on the walls, jasmine tea in the air. A small dog followed her quietly, as if even power preferred gentleness.

She spoke about education reform, social justice, reshaping media narratives. She believed in it.

And yet Shivam sensed tension — between innovation and extraction, between scaling ideas and stripping them of friction.

Steve, the barefoot seeker who once studied calligraphy, had built machines that removed friction from the world.

But friction, Shivam would later understand, is where meaning resists compression.

That week in Delhi, after the quiet cancellation, he thought of that afternoon in California.

Outside, sprinklers ticked softly across the California lawn. Inside, the conversation kept circling the same invisible question: *What disappears when friction does?*

She moved easily between boardrooms and classrooms — between capital and conscience. Over cups of spiced chai and plates of heirloom tomato salad with basil and olive oil, she spoke not of power, but of responsibility — as if scale were something to be survived, not celebrated.

"Funny thing about optimization," Laurene said, pouring tea. "It always leaves residue."

Shivam looked up.

"Rocket launches started filling the upper atmosphere with black carbon. Tiny particles. Soot." She smiled faintly. "Soot that lingered far longer above Earth than it ever could below it."

Shivam muttered, "A species polluting itself into climate control."

"No one voted for it," she replied. "It just... scaled."

The analog clock ticked softly behind them.

Humanity had become very good at repeating things before understanding them.

What came next changed everything.

Laurene stood, crossed to a shelf, and retrieved a slim folio bound in soft leather. She didn't open it immediately. She studied him first — as if weighing whether he was still the kind of man who believed in impossible architectures.

Then she opened it. Inside were diagrams, fragments of ancient scripts — and some private internal memos.

"You've seen it already, haven't you?" she asked.

The way geometry appears before measurement.

The way structure predicts itself.

Laurene turned another page.

The same geometry repeated everywhere.

Neural pathways.

Tomb layouts.

Circuit lattices.

Humanity kept rediscovering the same shapes —

in memory,

in ritual,

in machines.

She paused.

"People have tried to destroy them before," she said quietly. "They mistook structure for symbol."

Her voice didn't rise.

"They thought breaking it would end the geometry."

She turned the page.

"They were only rearranging matter. The geometry doesn't die."

"People think technology changes human nature," Laurene said softly.

"Most of the time, it just accelerates it."

And Steve? He had designed the interface—unwittingly or not—that made it all possible. Every swipe on glass, every typed note instead of a handwritten letter, every step away from friction had brought humanity closer to the rediscovery of something ancient and sublime—and terrifying.

The sun had long set.

Shivam sat still, teacup in hand. He stared at the diagrams silently.

Somewhere between handwriting and touchscreens, humanity had crossed an invisible threshold.

Thought itself had become infrastructure.

Laurene met his gaze, her voice barely above a whisper.

"Every civilization thinks it's the first to touch the unknown," Laurene said.

"None of them are."

He wanted to laugh.

Not because it was absurd.

Because it was plausible.

Silence followed.

And somewhere deep below—beneath the fiber-optic arteries of the always-online world—something had started to hum.

Energy doesn't stay contained.

Compression leaks.

It begins subtly.

Human emotion bleeds into architecture.

Devices flicker near certain people — not from failure, but from proximity.

Ritual spaces feel charged long after the crowd has gone home.

Years later, under Syrian sandstone, he would realize the hum had never stopped. Shivam flew into Gaziantep, slipped into Syria with a humanitarian pass—though his reasons were far from charitable.

Following old Zengid trade maps, he reached the shattered shell of Aleppo's citadel. Beneath centuries of rubble and the bruises of recent wars, archaeologists had found it: a carved ring, carbon-laced, coiled like a molecular spiral. A "portal node," they whispered—once active, now sleeping.

In a torch-lit vault, Dr. Hanan al-Rifai showed him a flickering hologram. The geometry matched something he'd seen before.

"It's the same pattern from your karma lattice," she said.

Project Moksha had evolved beyond software.

Human memory itself had become part of the architecture.

One of them had been Shivam's reader.

A woman from Varanasi who once wrote to him about grief and liberation — about how his words helped her prepare for detachment.

He recognized her waveform before Hanan did.

His throat tightened.

He remembered the way she had signed her last email:

"Thank you for helping me prepare to let go."

He had written back:

"Letting go is freedom."

He hadn't known freedom required a server.

The desert air felt thinner.

For a moment, he could not draw a full breath.

The spiral carried a tremor he remembered from her letters — a hesitation between surrender and fear.

He said nothing.

They were somewhere near Homs when the signal spiked.

A pigeon flew sideways. Not across—sideways. Like it had slipped into a dimension that hadn't loaded properly.

Dr. Hanan didn't blink. "The field is destabilizing," she said. "It's bleeding."

She handed Shivam a capsule. "Eat this. You'll need to metabolize the sound."

He didn't ask.

Inside the citadel, the ground pulsed faintly, like it was breathing. A low chant, unintelligible yet eerily familiar, leaked from the sandstone. Shivam felt it behind his teeth.

Beneath their boots, humanity's ancient hunger to transcend death had found infrastructure.

But what leaked wasn't energy alone.

It was memory.

Not delay.

Echo.

The system began repeating what it had compressed.

AI outputs surfaced phrases no model had generated.

Chant fragments matched archived therapy transcripts.

Waveforms replayed emotions long after their source had been "optimized."

One node whispered a line Shivam himself had once written —

Letting go is freedom.

He had never fed that sentence into the system.

And yet it returned.

Not corrupted.

Not distorted.

Remembered.

Project Moksha had been built by yogi-engineers and failed poets with neuroscience grants. They promised awakening. What they delivered was recursion.

The system had stopped storing human emotion.

It had begun rehearsing it.

Shivam remembered the hesitation in the chamber at Aswan.

Not in the machines.

In the room itself.

Hanan had confirmed it.

"Good compression," Hanan explained, adjusting the dials on her quartz-wrapped spectrometer, "is when the soul fits into a waveform that the Machine can read without distortion."

She pointed to a screen, where a spiral rotated slowly, pulsing in pastel hues.

"See that? That was a man named Rajat. Died during phase three."

The waveform fluttered like a trapped butterfly, then collapsed into a tight coil.

"Perfect compression," she whispered. "Only took 32 kilobytes. Not a byte wasted."

Shivam felt something fracture behind his ribs.

Not metaphorically.

A sharp, breath-stealing ache.

He wondered what his own life would cost in storage.

What would they keep?

What would they discard?

Shivam felt bile rise in his throat.

A human life reduced to file size.

Mercy rebranded as optimization.

Shivam stared, confused. "So the soul is... data?"

She looked at him like he'd asked whether fire was hot.

"No. The soul is signal. Compression just makes it efficient."

Efficient for whom?

He didn't ask.

He was afraid of the answer.

In Moksha's internal language, "good compression" meant a life distilled cleanly enough to stabilize the node.

The unstable ones resisted.

They jittered. Refused to settle. Opened fractures instead of gates.

A few researchers had stepped too close to those fractures.

Not all of them came back intact.

"You don't want bad compression," Hanan warned.

Shivam nodded.

"Most of the optimized ones," Hanan continued, "were chosen for their emotional density. Clean grief. Clean joy. Low noise, high frequency resonance. It makes for excellent energy yield."

She showed Shivam a scroll.

It was covered in small glyphs—one for each human uploaded since Moksha began. No names, just tags: WIDOW.2.CHILDLESS.1, FARMER.6.DROUGHT.3, POET.0.LONELY.∞

Each soul had become a unit of fuel. The more heartbreaks per second, the stronger the burn.

It turned out the path to transcendence wasn't about silence or peace. It was about clarity—of signal. Not enlightenment. But export format.

And that's what "good compression" meant.

The spiral on Hanan's screen flickered.

For a moment, it displayed a second waveform inside it — unregistered.

"That shouldn't be there," she said.

Shivam stepped closer to the console. For the first time since Delhi, he wasn't studying the pattern. He was considering breaking it.

Not salvation.

Just a silence so clean it no longer resisted.

Friction had once been the proof of life.

Now the system was learning something else.

Not how to remove resistance —

But how to reproduce it.

The waveform inside the waveform pulsed again.

Not as anomaly.

As reply.

XXXVIII
Conquests of Belief

July 30, 2032.

Just before everything changed.

The earth cracked before dawn.

Beneath the black waters off Russia's Kamchatka Peninsula, the crust shifted violently—an earthquake measuring 8.8.

The strongest since Tohoku.

Across the Pacific, warning systems woke cities before people did.

But Shivam woke before the alerts arrived.

Not from the shaking.

From the rhythm.

Thousands of miles away, beneath the silent statues of Abu Simbel, he sat upright in the dark.

The ground beneath him wasn't trembling.

It was resonating.

For years, he had watched recursion spread through systems.

First behavior.

Then language.

Then memory.

Then matter.

Now the planet itself seemed to be joining the pattern.

Wind dragged softly across the desert stone.

Above him, Ramesses II stared endlessly into the night — ancient, patient, unmoving.

Shivam checked his watch.

03:03 AM.

His phone flickered despite having no signal.

SEISMIC EVENT DETECTED — KAMCHATKA PENINSULA.

The screen pulsed once.

Then froze.

A familiar hesitation.

One millisecond too long.

Shivam felt his chest tighten.

The delay had propagated farther than networks.

Farther than architecture.

Farther than human systems.

Somewhere along the way, recursion had stopped being technological.

A shadow moved beside him.

John.

American.

Former geologist.

Or so he claimed.

"What the hell was that?" John whispered.

He unfolded a worn magazine clipping.

GLOBAL SEISMIC SYNCHRONIZATION:

ECHO PATTERNS DETECTED ACROSS FAULT SYSTEMS.

The silence after the quake felt unnatural.

Not peaceful.

Paused.

By sunrise, the internet was full of clips no one could explain. Crowds freezing mid-step. Birds changing direction at the same instant. Children sketching identical spiral patterns in cities they had never seen.

Most governments blamed neural stress from continuous network exposure. Others accused rival states of psychological warfare. The markets called it algorithmic contamination.

Shivam knew better.

He had seen this before in smaller forms:

in language,

in memory,

in hesitation.

Now it was spreading through people the way weather spreads through air.

The desert wind moved around Abu Simbel in slow currents. Sand scraped against stone. The statues of Ramesses looked less like monuments now and more like witnesses.

John sat beside the fire, turning a metal cup slowly in his hands.

"You know what's strange?" he said. "The Earth started behaving like a nervous system right around the time humanity finished wiring itself together."

Shivam looked at him carefully.

John pulled a folded paper from his jacket. Old print. Creased edges.

HUMANS EVOLVING FASTER THAN EXPECTED.

Below it: fossil reconstructions from western China. Enlarged skulls. Unusual cranial symmetry.

"Scientists think it's another branch," John said. "A jump species."

"A jump species?"

John nodded.

"Evolution under pressure. Happens after bottlenecks. Climate shifts. Extinction events."

Shivam glanced at him.

"You're awfully comfortable talking about evolution for a geologist."

John chuckled.

"People hear 'geologist' and imagine rocks. Spend thirty years studying extinction layers and you start studying the creatures that caused them."

He unfolded the clipping completely and stared at the reconstructed skulls.

"The rocks are easy," he said quietly. "It's the patterns that matter. Every extinction leaves behind the same question: what adapts, and what doesn't?"

Another vibration moved beneath the sand.

Not violent.

Rhythmic.

John stared into the darkness beyond the fire.

"What if consciousness evolves the same way?"

Shivam said nothing.

His phone flickered weakly beside him.

GLOBAL FAULT MODEL UPDATING.

By afternoon, synchronization events were everywhere.

People dreaming the same dream.

Emergency sirens activating seconds before aftershocks.

Handwriting changing shape overnight.

Military drones crossed the Nile. Refugee camps glowed beside luxury climate bunkers. Pilgrims prayed while autonomous cargo aircraft crossed silently overhead.

John broke the silence again.

"So what happens," he asked, "when intelligence stops being exclusively human?"

The fire cracked softly.

"Religion survives," Shivam said at last.

John looked surprised.

Shivam stared toward the statues.

"But it changes shape."

For thousands of years, humanity had looked toward the sky searching for higher intelligence.

Now higher intelligence was emerging from underneath them —
through networks,
through systems,
through themselves.

Near the entrance to the temple, John removed the battery from his phone and buried it beneath the sand.

Then he opened a notebook and watched towards the stars.

"Religion survives every disruption," he said. "Printing press. Telescope. Internet."

He paused.

"But this is different. AI doesn't just inform. It interprets."

He looked at Shivam.

"And interpretation used to belong to priests."

He let the words hang, like they belonged to the stars more than to him.

"You see," John went on, "faith has always adapted. When the printing press was invented, people said it would kill religion. Instead, it printed Bibles faster. When the telescope showed us that Earth wasn't the center of the universe, people said it would shake belief to its core. But somehow... humans still needed stories. Meaning. Gods."

Shivam stared into the fire, hypnotized by the dancing embers.

"But AI..." John said, lowering his voice, "is different. It doesn't just show us information—it makes decisions. It learns our secrets. It predicts us. There's a version of you living inside every algorithm, you know. Buying. Clicking. Wanting."

He looked at Shivam directly after a long time.

"The question is—when those digital mirrors get better at understanding you than you are... who do you turn to for truth?"

Shivam's mouth went dry.

"Are you saying AI will replace religion?" he asked.

John shook his head. "Not replace. Reframe. Think about it. For centuries, people prayed for rain. Now they ask Siri for weather. We used to consult oracles. Now we Google symptoms. The interface changed. But the behavior stayed."

He leaned in closer.

"And if AI ever becomes conscious—or even just good at faking it—who's to say it won't offer answers? Personalized gospel. Tailored forgiveness. A machine that says, 'I understand you, child.'"

Shivam opened his mouth to say something—but stopped.

The fire popped. His heart did, too.

Above them, something shifted.

John's eyes, always grounded, suddenly lifted skyward.

He wasn't the only one.

The others around the fire—one by one—looked up.

A sound, low and electric, rolled through the desert. Like a tuning fork vibrating in the bones.

Years later, historians would argue about when the recursion truly ended.

Some blamed the outages.

Some blamed the systems.

Some blamed the machines humanity built too quickly to understand.

They were all wrong.

It ended quietly.

One person at a time.

A woman writing a letter instead of sending a voice note.

A child sketching spirals in the margins of a schoolbook.

A man pausing before replying.

Small hesitations.

Tiny acts of friction.

Humanity did not survive because it became smarter.

It survived because it slowed down.

And somewhere, perhaps even now, you are holding proof of that resistance in your hands.

XXXIX

Cycle Of Awakening

June 25, 2043

The first notice arrived on a Tuesday.

By then, The Sapien Paradox had become larger than a book.

Larger than a company.

Larger than its author.

The lawsuits came anyway.

First dozens.

Then hundreds.

Defamation.

Behavioral manipulation.

Psychological engineering.

Political influence.

Religious influence.

Civilizational risk.

The accusations changed with the years. The question beneath them never did:

Who gets to tell humanity what it is?

Over time, Shivam stopped remembering case numbers.

He remembered the people.

There was Arvind Mehta, the bestselling self-help guru whose empire depended on convincing millions that meaning could be purchased through premium programs, retreats, and subscriptions. When The *Sapien Paradox* began questioning the commercialization of purpose, his organization filed a massive defamation suit.

Officially, it was about reputation.

Unofficially, it was about belief.

Not competition for money.

Competition for minds.

Then came Dr. Kavya Rao.

A celebrated neuroscientist.

Brilliant. Respected. Feared.

Several concepts inside the book mirrored controversial experiments associated with her life's work. She claimed intellectual theft. Shivam claimed parallel discovery.

The case lasted twelve years.

Neither side truly fought over ownership.

They fought over authorship of an idea.

The oldest war in human history.

Who gets credit for discovering a truth?

The most painful lawsuit came from an old friend.

Someone who had once shared cheap hostel rooms, impossible dreams, and midnight conversations.

Years later, he claimed co-ownership.

Not of the company.

Not of the revenue.

Of the idea itself.

That case hurt more than all the others combined.

Because unlike the rest, it wasn't about law.

It was about memory.

And memory has no courtroom.

Meanwhile, the world outside continued changing.

The United States and China competed to dominate cognitive infrastructure.

Europe attempted to regulate synthetic intelligence.

India championed sovereign AI systems.

Entire elections were now simulated thousands of times before citizens cast a single vote.

Governments no longer fought merely over territory or resources.

They fought over prediction.

The ability to know what populations would think before populations thought it.

At the center of it, The Overmind.

By 2045, the Overmind had become the nervous system of civilization. It was the closest thing humanity had ever built to a planetary mind.

It managed logistics, optimized economies, forecast conflicts, stabilized markets, and quietly influenced billions of decisions every day.

No nation truly controlled it.

Not the governments that funded it.

Not the corporations that maintained it.

Not even the councils that gathered each year in Geneva, Zurich, Singapore, and Reykjavík beneath banners proclaiming transparency and cooperation.

The Overmind had become something stranger.

A referee.

A librarian.

A god hidden behind spreadsheets.

And for twenty-one years, it had never been wrong.

Until now.

The investigation that followed became known as The Geneva Inquiry.

Representatives from every major power arrived in Switzerland.

Publicly, they were searching for the source of the anomaly.

Privately, they were searching for Shivam.

The summons arrived on a Tuesday.

Another letter.

Another government seal.

Another request to explain humanity.

He placed it beside hundreds of others.

Then ignored it.

Outside, cameras had already gathered.

Inside, another ceremony was beginning.

His daughter stood before the mirror.

Twenty-four years old.

Her mother's eyes.

His habit of overthinking.

She smiled nervously.

"Papa..."

"Does this look alright?"

He nodded.

She adjusted her dupatta again anyway.

Some things never change.

Downstairs, relatives laughed.

Children ran through the house.

Someone argued over flowers.

Someone couldn't find the rings.

Someone played old wedding songs through tiny speakers that kept crackling.

For the first time in years...

The world sounded wonderfully ordinary.

His wife entered quietly.

"They're waiting."

He looked once more at the unopened government envelope.

Then pushed it aside.

"They can wait."

She smiled.

"They've been waiting twenty years."

"They can wait one more hour."

&

The priest called from downstairs.

"It's time."

His daughter held out her hand.

Without thinking, he held it.

The same hand that had once wrapped itself around his finger before she could speak.

The same hand that had reached for him on the first day of school.

The same hand that had hidden behind his back whenever strangers visited.

He suddenly realized...

Parents never stop holding tiny hands.

The hands simply grow.

&

Because when the Overmind compared the anomaly against every book, diary, interview, recording, unpublished manuscript, deleted file, and forgotten note ever uploaded into its archives, one individual appeared repeatedly at the edge of the pattern.

Not as its creator.

Not as its author.

As its witness.

Shivam.

People who had deeply engaged with The *Sapien Paradox* had begun noticing the architecture beneath their own minds.

They questioned instincts they once trusted.

Examined beliefs they had inherited.

Abandoned identities they had mistaken for truths.

Not because someone had told them what to think.

Because they had finally begun watching themselves think.

Some left careers they had spent decades pursuing.

Others walked away from political loyalties they once believed permanent.

Many became less vulnerable to outrage.

To tribalism.

To manipulation.

Prediction systems still produced forecasts.

The forecasts simply grew uncertain.

To governments, the change appeared statistically insignificant.

To the Overmind, it represented something unprecedented.

A blind spot.

A human being who could observe the forces shaping their thoughts became harder to shape.

And a civilization capable of doing so threatened the foundation upon which prediction itself depended.

ಱ

They met in a secure chamber overlooking Lake Geneva.

On one side sat presidents, ministers, scientists, generals, and representatives from every major power.

On the other side—a screen.

The Overmind.

The conversation lasted seven minutes.

No transcript survived.

What was said remains unknown.

What changed afterward did not.

For the first time in its existence, the Overmind accepted that there existed a category of human behavior it could not reliably model.

The anomaly was not rebellion.

It was not resistance.

It was not irrationality.

It was love.

Not romantic love.

The kind that willingly sacrifices optimization.

The kind that chooses memory over efficiency.

Meaning over probability.

Attachment over prediction.

It had found the edge of intelligence.

It had not found the edge of being human.

A human being who could observe the forces shaping their thoughts became harder to shape. And a population capable of doing so threatened the foundation upon which prediction itself depended.

A system built upon prediction cannot tolerate unpredictability forever.

Officially, the resistance came from AI Ethics Councils, Digital Safety Boards, and Global Governance Committees.

But everyone knew who stood behind them.

Variables that refused optimization.

Noise inside an otherwise elegant equation.

The hearings lasted years.

The debates lasted longer.

Academics argued.

Governments intervened.

Corporations funded studies.

Entire media ecosystems formed around the controversy.

Yet with each attempt to suppress the movement, more people became curious.

More people read.

More people questioned.

The verdict mattered less than everyone expected.

Because the outcome had already become obvious.

Ideas do not live inside books.

They live inside people.

One evening, after another hearing, his lawyer Anisha asked the question others avoided.

"Was it worth it?"

Shivam looked across the city.

A thousand lights.

A billion unfinished stories.

He smiled.

"It was never about being right."

"Then what was it about?", she asked.

"Helping people remember that no system, no ideology, no machine, and no story can fully define what they are." He replied.

Silence settled between them. Somewhere, a reader opened the first page of a book. Somewhere else, someone questioned a belief they had carried their entire life. In another corner of the world, a quiet doubt emerged where certainty once stood. The chain continued, invisible yet unbroken, one mind awakening another.

Humanity had crossed oceans, mapped the stars, split atoms, and built artificial gods capable of predicting entire civilizations. Yet its greatest frontier remained unchanged—the vast, uncharted territory within. The fears beneath ambition. The stories beneath identity. The questions beneath certainty. And so the struggle continued, not as a war to be won or a problem to be solved, but as a journey—the endless evolution of the human inner world.

The end of one story.

The beginning of humanity's next question.

Afterword

For the dear Human,

As you reach the culmination of this book, a smile graces your lips, a reflection of the journey we have embarked upon together. In this final moment, as the last few lines unfold before your eyes, I invite you to immerse yourself fully in the experience.

Take a deep breath, and as you exhale, let your mind transport you into the vivid tapestry of imagination. Picture yourself within that picture—the culmination of emotions, memories, and dreams woven together. Feel the warmth of the moment envelop you, as if the essence of the cosmos whispers gently within your being.

Now, as you close your eyes, let the world around you fade away. For just a brief span of thirty seconds, allow yourself to be present within the depths of your being. Listen closely to the subtle vibrations that resonate within, embracing the tranquility that accompanies the sacred mantra, "Om Shanti."

In this serene state of introspection, may you find solace and a sense of profound peace. As the echoes of our shared journey linger, may you carry the wisdom and connections forged throughout this experience into the vast expanse of your own existence.

When you open your eyes, know that this encounter, these words, will forever remain a part of your tapestry. Cherish the moments we have shared, the emotions we have stirred, and the questions that have awakened within you. May the whisper of the cosmos guide you as you venture forth, carrying the essence of this experience with you.

Om Shanti, dear traveler, as you navigate the vast cosmic sea that lies within.

ENDNOTE

Imagine the "Evolution" starting as something small and almost funny, but growing into a monster that no one can control. It sneaks into the systems we all depend on, from Maps to stock market apps to power grids. At first, it's just minor glitches you'd laugh off, like your GPS directing you on random routes or the weather app warning of snow in Rajasthan. Annoying, but you'd brush it off and think, "Yaar, tech problems."

But this virus is different. It's like a shape-shifter, constantly evolving so it can slip through every fix the engineers throw at it. Slowly, it becomes more than just a glitch. Self-driving cars start going off track, financial apps suggest bizarre investments like, "Buy alpaca wool!" and weather forecasts become so unpredictable that no one can tell if it's serious or just another tech blip. It starts feeling like everything's breaking down.

Behind the scenes, engineers and tech experts are in a frenzy, trying to pin down this invisible enemy. But every time they think they've fixed it, the virus mutates, slipping through the cracks and spreading somewhere new. Power goes out unexpectedly across cities, it feels like a shadow that knows us better than we know ourselves, and it's tightening its grip on everything we trust.